LUCIAN'S
JUDGMENT OF THE GODDESSES

An Intermediate Greek Reader

Greek Text with Running Vocabulary and Commentary

D1715637

Evan Hayes
and
Stephen Nimis

Lucian's *Judgment of the Goddesses*: An Intermediate Greek Reader: Greek Text with Running Vocabulary and Commentary

First Edition

Updated June 2016

© 2015 by Evan Hayes and Stephen Nimis

All rights reserved. Subject to the exception immediately following, this book may not be reproduced, in whole or in part, in any form (beyond copying permitted by Sections 107 and 108 of the U.S. Copyright Law and except by reviewers for the public press), without written permission from the publisher. The authors have made a version of this work available (via email) under a Creative Commons Attribution-Noncommercial-Share Alike 3.0 License. The terms of the license can be accessed at www.creativecommons.org.

Accordingly, you are free to copy, alter and distribute this work under the following conditions:

1. You must attribute the work to the author (but not in a way that suggests that the author endorses your alterations to the work).

2. You may not use this work for commercial purposes.

3. If you alter, transform or build up this work, you may distribute the resulting work only under the same or similar license as this one.

ISBN-10: 1940997127

ISBN-13: 9781940997124

Published by Faenum Publishing, Ltd.

Cover Design: Evan Hayes

Fonts: Garamond
          GFS Porson

editor@faenumpublishing.com

TABLE OF CONTENTS

matri carae
Sherena Chapman Hayes

Acknowledgments

The idea for this project grew out of work that we, the authors, did with support from Miami University's Undergraduate Summer Scholars Program, for which we thank Martha Weber and the Office of Advanced Research and Scholarship. Work on the series, of which this volume is a part, was generously funded by the Joanna Jackson Goldman Memorial Prize through the Honors Program at Miami University. We owe a great deal to Carolyn Haynes, and the 2010 Honors & Scholars Program Advisory Committee for their interest and confidence in the project.

The technical aspects of the project were made possible through the invaluable advice and support of Bill Hayes, Christopher Kuo, and Daniel Meyers. The equipment and staff of Miami University's Interactive Language Resource Center were a great help along the way. We are also indebted to the Perseus Project, especially Gregory Crane and Bridget Almas, for their technical help and resources. We also profited greatly from advice and help on the POD process from Geoffrey Steadman.

Special thanks are due to Tom Garvey, who reviewed the text and pointed out numerous errors which we were able to address in this updated edition. All responsibility for errors, however, rests with the authors themselves.

INTRODUCTION

The aim of this book is to make *The Judgment of the Goddeses* by Lucian of Samosata (c. 120 CE –190) accessible to intermediate students of Ancient Greek. The running vocabulary and grammatical commentary are meant to provide everything necessary to read each page, so that readers can progress through the text, improving their knowledge of Greek while enjoying one of the most entertaining authors of antiquity.

Lucian's *The Judgment of the Goddeses* is one of Lucian's shorter works and is a great text for intermediate readers. It is in dialogue form and fun to read, with few complicated sentences. The dialogue relates the story of Paris' fateful decision to award first prize to Aphrodite in a beauty contest. Aphrodite had promised Paris the most beautiful woman in the world (Helen, the wife of Menelaus) as a bride if he chose Aphrodite. This becomes the cause of the Trojan War, the greatest of the classical epic stories. In typical fashion, Lucian presents the characters in the story humorously, the goddesses as well as Paris. Each of the goddesses tries to pry some information about Paris out of Hermes, complains about the unfair practices of the others, and shamelessly bribes the judge. For his part Paris is interested only in the relative value of the bribes, but this does not prevent him from insisting that he inspect each of three beauties naked. There are hints of the relentless hostility that Athena and Hera, the two losers in the contest, will come to hold toward the Trojans in the epic tradition.

The judgment of Paris was a favorite theme in art, appearing as early as the 7th c. BCE on a dedication by Cypselus of Corinth at Olympia, which showed Hermes presenting the three goddesses to Paris. This is described by Pausanias along with an inscription (5.18.7). There are a number of vases treating the theme, as well as paintings in the renaissance, where the opportunity to present three naked women made it popular. There is an elaborate description of a mime performance of the judgment in Apuleius' *The Golden Ass* (10.29-34) accompanied by an apostrophe to the reader denouncing bribery in the courts. See also Ovid, *Heroides* 16 (Paris to Helen).

Little is known about the life of Lucian except what can be deduced from his numerous surviving works. By his own account, he was a professional rhetor, a "sophist," trained in public speaking. As such he is a good representative of the renaissance of Greek literature in the imperial period known as the "Second

Sophistic." His Greek prose is patterned on the best Attic authors, a learned version of Greek that was more prestigious than the living *lingua franca* of the time, *koine* Greek, the Greek of the *New Testament* and public administration in the eastern half of the Roman Empire.

The Greek text is that of K. Jacobitz (1896), which has been digitized by the Perseus Project and made available with a Creative Commons license, as is our text. Jacobitz printed this dialogue as Number 20 in the *Dialogues of the Gods*, but the work is different from those dialogues in many ways, and modern editors print it as an independent work.

Select Bibliography

Bartley, Adam. "Techniques of Composition in Lucian's Minor Dialogues." *Hermes* 133.3 (2005), 358-367.

Branham, R. Bracht. *Unruly Eloquence: Lucian and the Comedy of Traditions.* Harvard University Press: Cambridge, 1987.

Deferrari, R. J. *Lucian's Atticism.* Hackert: Amsterdam, 1969.

Dickie, Matthew. "Lucian's Gods" edd. J. N. Bremmer and A. Erskine, *The Gods of Ancient Greece* (Edinburgh: Edinburgh University Press, 2010), 348-61.

Householder, F. W. *Literary Quotation and Allusion in Lucian.* King's Crown Press: Morningside Heights, 1941.

Pötscher, Walter. "Athene-Mythen und ihre Behandlung bei Lukian: θεῶν διάλογοι 13 (8) und Θεῶν κρίσις 10." *Würzburg Jahrbücher für dir Altertumswissenschaft* 21 (1996-1997), 309-317.

How to use this book

The page-by-page vocabularies gloss all but the most common words. We have endeavored to make these glossaries as useful as possible without becoming fulsome. Words occurring frequently in the text can be found in an appendix in the back, but it is our hope that most readers will not need to use this appendix often.

The commentary is almost exclusively grammatical, explaining subordinate clauses, unusual verb forms, and idioms. Brief summaries of a number of grammatical and morphological topics are interspersed through the text as well, and there is a list of verbs used by Lucian that have unusual forms in an appendix. The principal parts of those verbs are given there rather than in the glossaries.

An Important Disclaimer:

This volume is a self-published "Print on Demand" (POD) book, and it has not been vetted or edited in the usual way by publishing professionals. There are sure to be some factual and typographical errors in the text, for which we apologize in advance. The volume is also available only through online distributors, since each book is printed when ordered online. However, this publishing channel and format also account for the low price of the book, and it is a simple matter to make changes when they come to our attention. For this reason, any corrections or suggestions for improvement are welcome and will be addressed as quickly as possible in future versions of the text.

Please e-mail corrections or suggestions to editor@faenumpublishing.com.

About the Authors:

Evan Hayes is a graduate in Classics and Philosophy at Miami University and the 2011 Joanna Jackson Goldman Scholar.

Stephen Nimis is Emeritus Professor of Classics at Miami University and Professor of English and Comparative Literature at the American University in Cairo.

Abbreviations

abs.	absolute	m.	masculine
acc.	accusative	mid.	middle
act.	active	neg.	negative
adj.	adjective	neut.	neuter
adv.	adverb	nom.	nominative
aor.	aorist	obj.	object
app.	apposition	opt.	optative
artic.	articular	part.	participle
attrib.	attributive	pass.	passive
circum.	circumstantial	perf.	perfect
com.	command	pl.	plural
comp.	comparison	plupf.	pluperfect
dat.	dative	pot.	potential
delib.	deliberative	pred.	predicate
f.	feminine	pres.	present
fut.	future	pron.	pronoun
gen.	genitive	purp.	purpose
i.e.	*id est* ("that is")	quest.	question
imper.	imperative	s.	singular
impf.	imperfect	sc.	*scilicet* ("supply")
ind.	indirect	st.	statement
indic.	indicative	subj.	subjunctive
inf.	infinitive	suppl.	supplementary
intr.	intransitive	voc.	vocative

ΛΟΥΚΙΑΝΟΥ
ΘΕΩΝ ΚΡΙΣΙΣ

Lucian's
The Judgment of the Goddesses

ΘΕΩΝ ΚΡΙΣΙΣ

ΖΕΥΣ: Ἑρμῆ, λαβὼν τουτὶ τὸ μῆλον ἄπιθι εἰς τὴν Φρυγίαν παρὰ τὸν Πριάμου παῖδα τὸν βουκόλον — νέμει δὲ τῆς Ἴδης ἐν τῷ Γαργάρῳ — καὶ λέγε πρὸς αὐτόν, ὅτι «Σέ, ὦ Πάρι, κελεύει ὁ Ζεύς, ἐπειδὴ καλός τε αὐτὸς εἶ καὶ σοφὸς τὰ ἐρωτικά, δικάσαι ταῖς θεαῖς, ἥτις αὐτῶν ἡ καλλίστη

βουκόλος, ὁ: a shepherd
Γάργαρον, τό: the southern peak of Mt. Ida
δικάζω: to judge
Ἑρμῆς, -οῦ, ὁ: Hermes
ἐρωτικός, -ή, -όν: amatory
καλός, -η, -ον: handsome, beautiful
κελεύω: to command, order

λαμβάνω: to take
μῆλον, τό: apple
νέμω: to tend a pasture
παῖς, παῖδος, ὁ: a child
Πρίαμος, ὁ: Priam, father of Paris
σοφός, -ή, -όν: cunning
Φρυγία, ἡ: Phrygia

λαβών: aor. part. of λαμβάνω, "once having taken, depart" i.e. take it and depart"
ἄπιθι: pres. imper. of ἀπο-έρχομαι, "depart!"
τὰ ἐρωτικά: acc. of respect, "wise in erotic matters"
δικάσαι: aor. inf. in ind. command after κελεύει, "orders you to judge" + dat.

Note the different meanings of the word αὐτὸς:

1. The nominative forms of the word without the definite article are always intensive (= Latin ipse): αὐτὸς: he himself; αὐτοί, they themselves.

ἐπειδὴ καλός τε αὐτὸς εἶ: "since you yourself are handsome"

The other cases of the word are also intensive when they modify a noun or pronoun, either without the definite article or in predicative position:

ὥρα δὲ ἤδη καὶ ὑμῖν αὐταῖς ἀπιέναι παρὰ τὸν δικαστήν: "it is already time for you yourselves to go before the judge"

εἰ καὶ τὸν Μῶμον αὐτὸν ἐπιστήσειας: "even if you choose Momus himself"

2. Oblique cases of the word, when used without a noun or a definite article, are the unemphatic third person pronouns: him, them, etc.:

ἥτις αὐτῶν ἡ καλλίστη ἐστίν: "who of these is most beautiful"

δοκεῖ τις αὐτῷ συνοικεῖν Ἰδαία γυνή: "some Idaean woman seems to live with him"

3. Any case of the word with an article in attributive position means "the same":

ὁ γὰρ αὐτὸς ἄμφω ἦμεν. "We are both the same."

ἐστίν· τοῦ δὲ ἀγῶνος τὸ ἆθλον ἡ νικῶσα λαβέτω τὸ
μῆλον.» ὥρα δὲ ἤδη καὶ ὑμῖν αὐταῖς ἀπιέναι παρὰ τὸν
δικαστήν· ἐγὼ γὰρ ἀπωθοῦμαι τὴν δίαιταν ἐπ᾽ ἴσης τε
ὑμᾶς ἀγαπῶν, καὶ εἴ γε οἷόν τε ἦν, ἡδέως ἂν ἁπάσας
νενικηκυίας ἰδών. ἄλλως τε καὶ ἀνάγκη, μιᾷ τὸ καλλιστεῖον ἀποδόντα πάντως ἀπεχθάνεσθαι ταῖς πλείοσιν.
διὰ ταῦτα αὐτὸς μὲν οὐκ ἐπιτήδειος ὑμῖν δικαστής, ὁ δὲ
νεανίας οὗτος ὁ Φρὺξ ἐφ᾽ ὃν ἄπιτε βασιλικὸς μέν ἐστι

ἀγαπάω: to love, be fond of
ἀγών, ἀγῶνος, ὁ: a contest brought
ἆθλον, τό: the prize of contest
ἄλλως: in another way or manner
ἀνάγκη, ἡ: force, necessity
ἀπεχθάνομαι: to incur hatred (+ dat.)
ἀποδίδωμι: to give back, render
ἀπωθέω: to thrust away, push back
βασιλικός, -ή, -όν: royal, kingly
δίαιτα, ἡ: an arbitration, suit
δικαστής, -οῦ, ὁ: a judge

εἷς, μία, ἕν: one
ἐπιτήδειος, -α, -ον: suitable, convenient
ἡδέως: sweetly
ἴσος, -η, -ον: equal to, the same as
καλλιστεῖον, τό: the prize of beauty
νικάω: to conquer, win
οἷος τε εἰμί: to be able to (+ inf.)
πάντως: altogether
πλέων, -ον: more
ὥρα, ἡ: period of time

τὸ ἆθλον: acc. pred., "an apple *as a prize*"
λαβέτω: aor. 3 s. imper., "let her take!"
ὥρα δὲ: "*it is time* for you..." these words are addressed to the goddesses themselves
ἀπιέναι: pres. inf. of ἀπο-έρχομαι epexegetic after ὥρα, "time *to go*"
ἐπ᾽ ἴσης: adverbial, "loving you *equally*"
ἀγαπῶν: pres. part. causal, "*because loving* you", i.e. "because I love you"
εἴ γε οἷόν τε ἦν: impf. in present contrafactual protasis, "if it were possible"
ἡδέως ἂν ... ἰδών: aor. part. serving as future less vivid apodosis replacing an aor. opt.
   (ἴδοιμι), "I should be glad to see you"
νενικηκυίας: perf. part. acc. f. in ind. st. after ἰδών, "see *that all have won*"
ἄλλως τε καὶ: "otherwise and also" i.e. especially because
ἀποδόντα: aor. part. acc. agreeing with με understood, the subject of ἀπεχθάνεσθαι,
   "that I *having given* the prize"
αὐτὸς μὲν ... ὁ δὲ: "while I myself ... this youth"
ἄπιτε: fut. of ἀπο-έρχομαι, "to whom *you will go*"

καὶ Γανυμήδους τουτουὶ συγγενής, τὰ ἄλλα δὲ ἀφελὴς
καὶ ὄρειος, κοὐκ ἄν τις αὐτὸν ἀπαξιώσειε τοιαύτης θέας.

ΑΦΡΟΔΙΤΗ: Ἐγὼ μέν, ὦ Ζεῦ, εἰ καὶ τὸν Μῶμον αὐτὸν
ἐπιστήσειας ἡμῖν δικαστήν, θαρροῦσα βαδιοῦμαι πρὸς
τὴν ἐπίδειξιν· τί γὰρ ἂν καὶ μωμήσαιτό μου; χρὴ δὲ καὶ
ταύταις ἀρέσκειν τὸν ἄνθρωπον.

ἀπαξιόω: to deem unworthy
ἀρέσκω: to be pleasing
ἀφελής, -ές: simple
βαδίζω: to go slowly, to walk
ἐπίδειξις, -εως, ἡ: a proof, demonstration
ἐφίστημι: to set upon, establish
θαρρέω: to be of good courage

θέα, ἡ: a seeing, looking at, view
μωμάομαι: to blame
Μῶμος, ὁ: Momus
ὄρειος, -α, -ον: of the mountains
συγγενής, -ές: born with, congenital
τοιοῦτος, -αύτη, -οῦτο: such as this
χρή: it is fated, necessary

Γανυμήδους: gen., "a relative *of Ganymede*," the son of Tros
ἀπαξιώσειε: aor. opt. pot., "no one *would deem unworthy of*" + gen.
Μῶμον: the god of blame who appears prominently in Lucian's *Council of the Gods*
ἐπιστήσειας: aor. opt. of ἐπι-ἵστημι in future less vivid protasis, "even if *you were to establish*"
βαδιοῦμαι: fut. in future more vivid apodosis, "I will go"
μωμήσαιτο: aor. opt. pot., "what could he blame?"
τὸν ἄνθρωπον: acc. subject of ἀρέσκειν, "*that the man* be pleasing to" + dat.

Future Conditions

The **future more vivid** condition indicates a future action as a *probability*.

The **future less vivid** condition indicates a future action as a *possibility*;

more vivid: ἐάν (Attic contraction = ἤν or ἄν) plus subjunctive in the protasis, future indicative or equivalent in the apodosis: in English "if he does this ... then he will...."

less vivid: εἰ plus optative in the protasis, ἄν plus the optative in the apodosis: in English: "If he were to... then he would..."

> ἢν γάρ με, ὦ Πάρι, δικάσῃς εἶναι καλήν, ἀπάσης ἔσῃ τῆς Ἀσίας δεσπότης. "*For if you judge me* to be beautiful, Paris, *you will be* master of Asia."

But Lucian sometimes uses the optative in the protasis with a future indicative in the apodosis:

> εἰ καὶ τὸν Μῶμον αὐτὸν ἐπιστήσειας ἡμῖν δικαστήν, θαρροῦσα βαδιοῦμαι πρὸς τὴν ἐπίδειξιν· "*Even if you were to appoint* Momus as our judge, *I will* boldly *proceed* to the demonstration."

ΗΡΑ: Οὐδ' ἡμεῖς, ὦ Ἀφροδίτη, δέδιμεν, οὐδ' ἂν ὁ Ἄρης ὁ σὸς
ἐπιτραπῇ τὴν δίαιταν· ἀλλὰ δεχόμεθα καὶ τοῦτον, ὅστις
ἂν ᾖ, τὸν Πάριν.

Ἄρης, ὁ: Ares
δέδια: to fear (*perf.*)
δέχομαι: to take, accept, receive

δίαιτα, ἡ: arbitration, suit
ἐπιτρέπω: to turn to, trust (an arbitration)
to (+ *dat.*)

δέδιμεν: perf. with present meaning, "we fear"

οὐδ' ἂν ... ἐπιτραπῇ: aor. subj. pass. in present general protasis, "*not even if* Ares *were
entrusted* the suit"

ὅστις ἂν ᾖ: pres. subj. in general relative clause, "whoever he is"

Endings of the Second Person Singular Middle

The regular middle-passive endings in the singular are as follows:

primary	secondary
-μαι	-μην
-σαι	-σο
-ται	-το

The endings of the second person middle (-σαι, -σο) undergo changes when
preceded by the thematic vowel -ε- in the conjugation of verbs like παύομαι.
Specifically, the intervocalic -σ- drops out and the vowels contract: εσαι → εαι → η
(sometimes spelled ει) and εσο → εο → ου. Compare the following:

κεῖμαι	παύομαι	ἐκείμην	ἐπαυόμην
κεῖσαι	παύῃ	ἐκείσο	ἐπαύου
κεῖται	παύεται	ἐκεῖτο	ἐπαύετο

Contract verbs undergo further changes in the present system, producing an ending
that can sometimes be confused with active endings.

θεῶμαι	ποιοῦμαι	δηλοῦμαι	ἐθεώμην	ἐποιούμην	ἐδηλούμην
θεᾷ	ποιῇ	δηλοῖ	ἐθεῶ	ἐποιοῦ	ἐδηλοῦ
θεᾶται	ποιεῖται	δηλοῦται	ἐθέατο	ἐποιεῖτο	ἐδηλοῦτο

Particularly noteworthy is that the 2 s. middle primary ending is identical to the 3
s. active ending of the subjunctive, in both contract and uncontracted verbs.

Note also the effect of the loss of intervocalic -σ- in the present middle imperative
of contract verbs:

τιμάε-σο	→	τιμά-εο	→	τιμῶ
ποιέ-εσο	→	ποιέ-εο	→	ποιοῦ
δηλό-εσο	→	δηλό-εο	→	δηλοῦ

and the first aorist of παύομαι: ἐπαύσα-σο → ἐπαύσα-ο → ἐπαύσω

ΖΕΥΣ: Ἦ καὶ σοὶ ταῦτα, ὦ θύγατερ, συνδοκεῖ; τί φής; ἀποστρέφῃ καὶ ἐρυθριᾷς; ἔστι μὲν ἴδιον τὸ αἰδεῖσθαι τὰ τοιαῦτα ὑμῶν τῶν παρθένων· ἐπινεύεις δ᾽ ὅμως. ἄπιτε οὖν καὶ μὴ χαλεπήνητε τῷ δικαστῇ αἱ νενικημέναι μηδὲ κακὸν ἐντρίψησθε τῷ νεανίσκῳ· οὐ γὰρ οἷόν τε ἐπ᾽ ἴσης πάσας εἶναι καλάς.

ΕΡΜΗΣ: Προΐωμεν εὐθὺ τῆς Φρυγίας, ἐγὼ μὲν ἡγούμενος, ὑμεῖς δὲ μὴ βραδέως ἀκολουθεῖτέ μοι καὶ θαρρεῖτε. οἶδα ἐγὼ τὸν Πάριν. νεανίας ἐστὶ καλὸς καὶ τἆλλα ἐρωτικὸς

αἰδέομαι: to be ashamed to do, to be modest
ἀκολουθέω: to follow
ἀποστρέφω: to turn
βραδύς, -εῖα, -ύ: slow
ἐντρίβω: to rub in or into (+ *dat.*)
ἐπινεύω: to nod
ἐρυθριάω: to blush, to colour up
ἐρωτικός, -ή, -όν: amatory
εὐθύ: straight towards (+ *gen.*)
ἦ: in truth, truly
ἡγέομαι: to go before, lead the way
θαρρέω: to be of good courage

θυγάτηρ, θυγατρός, ἡ: a daughter
ἴδιος, -α, -ον: one's own, proper to (+ *gen.*)
κακός, -ή, -όν: bad
νεανίας, ὁ: a young man
νεάνισκος, ὁ: youth, young man
νικάω: to conquer, prevail, vanquish
οἷος τε εἰμι: to be able to (+ *inf.*)
παρθένος, ἡ: a maid, virgin
συνδοκέω: to seem good also
τοιοῦτος, -αύτη, -οῦτο: such as this
φημί: to declare, make known
χαλεπαίνω: to sore, grievous

ἦ καὶ: indicating an animated question, "and also to you?"

ἀποστρέφῃ: pres. 2 s. mid., "do you turn away?"

τὸ αἰδεῖσθαι: articular inf., "the being modest"

τὰ τοιαῦτα: acc. of respect, "modest *in such matters*"

δ᾽ ὅμως: "*but even so* you nod"

μὴ χαλεπήνητε: aor. subj. in prohibition, "don't complain about!" + dat.

αἱ νενικημέναι: perf. part., "those of you who have been defeated"

μηδὲ ... ἐντρίψησθε: aor. subj. in prohibition, "*and don't rub* some evil on him" i.e. don't cause him harm

οἷόν τε (sc. ἐστι): "for it is not possible" + inf.

καλάς: acc. pred., "all to be equally *beautiful*"

προΐωμεν: pres. subj. of προ-έρχομαι hortatory, "let's go!"

7

καὶ τὰ τοιαῦτα κρίνειν ἱκανώτατος. οὐκ ἂν ἐκεῖνος
δικάσειεν κακῶς.

ΑΦΡΟΔΙΤΗ: Τοῦτο μὲν ἄπαν ἀγαθὸν καὶ πρὸς ἐμοῦ λέγεις,
τὸ δίκαιον ἡμῖν εἶναι τὸν δικαστήν· πότερα δὲ ἄγαμός
ἐστιν οὗτος ἢ καὶ γυνή τις αὐτῷ σύνεστιν;

ΕΡΜΗΣ: Οὐ παντελῶς ἄγαμος, ὦ Ἀφροδίτη.

ΑΦΡΟΔΙΤΗ: Πῶς λέγεις;

ΕΡΜΗΣ: Δοκεῖ τις αὐτῷ συνοικεῖν Ἰδαία γυνή, ἱκανὴ μέν,
ἀγροῖκος δὲ καὶ δεινῶς ὄρειος, ἀλλ᾽ οὐ σφόδρα προσέχειν
αὐτῇ ἔοικε. τίνος δ᾽ οὖν ἕνεκα ταῦτα ἐρωτᾷς;

ΑΦΡΟΔΙΤΗ: Ἄλλως ἠρόμην.

ΑΘΗΝΑ: Παραπρεσβεύεις, ὦ οὗτος, ἰδίᾳ πάλαι ταύτῃ κοι-
νολογούμενος.

ἀγαθός, -ή, -όν: good
ἄγαμος, -ον: unmarried
ἀγροῖκος, -ον: of or in the country
ἄλλως: in another way or manner
γυνή, γυναικός, ἡ: a woman
δεινός, -ή, -όν: fearful, terrible
δικάζω: to judge, to give judgment on
δίκαιος, -α, -ον:: just
ἕνεκα: on account of (+ gen.)
ἔοικα: to seem, to be like
ἐρωτάω: to ask
Ἰδαῖος, -α, -ον: of Ida
ἴδιος, -α, -ον: one's own

ἱκανός, -ή, -όν: becoming, sufficient
κοινολογέομαι: to take counsel with (+ dat.)
κρίνω: to judge
ὄρειος, -ον: of or from the mountains
πάλαι: long ago
παντελής, -ές: complete, entire
παραπρεσβεύω: to execute an embassy
dishonestly
ποτερά … ἤ: "whether … or"
προσέχω: to hold to, be devoted to
σύνειμι: to be together, consort
συνοικέω: to dwell together
σφόδρα: very, very much

κρίνειν: pres. inf. epexegetic after ἱκανώτατος, "most suitable *to judge*"
οὐκ ἂν … δικάσειεν: aor. opt. pot., "he would not judge"
τοῦτο … λέγεις: "this (which) you say"
τὸ … εἶναι: articular inf. in apposition to τοῦτο, "namely, the judge *being* just"
ἱκανὴ μέν, ἀγροῖκος δὲ: "adequate but rustic"
προσέχειν: pres. inf. after ἔοικε, "he does not seem *to be devoted to*" + dat.
ἄλλως ἠρόμην: aor., "I asked otherwise" i.e. for no reason
ὦ οὗτος: vocative, "you there!"
ἰδίᾳ: dat. of manner, "taking counsel with *privately*"

ΕΡΜΗΣ: Οὐδέν, ὦ Ἀθηνᾶ, δεινὸν οὐδὲ καθ' ὑμῶν, ἀλλ' ἤρετό με εἰ ἄγαμος ὁ Πάρις ἐστίν.

ΑΘΗΝΑ: Ὡς δὴ τί τοῦτο πολυπραγμονοῦσα;

ΕΡΜΗΣ: Οὐκ οἶδα· φησὶ δ' οὖν ὅτι ἄλλως ἐπελθόν, οὐκ ἐξεπίτηδες ἤρετο.

ΑΘΗΝΑ: Τί οὖν; ἄγαμός ἐστιν;

ΕΡΜΗΣ: Οὐ δοκεῖ.

ΑΘΗΝΑ: Τί δέ; τῶν πολεμικῶν ἐστιν αὐτῷ ἐπιθυμία καὶ φιλόδοξός τις, ἢ τὸ πᾶν βουκόλος;

βουκόλος, ὁ: shepherd
δεινός, -ή, -όν: fearful, terrible
ἐξεπίτηδης, -ες: suitable
ἐπέρχομαι: to approach

ἐπιθυμία, ἡ: desire, yearning
πολεμικός, -ή, -όν: of or for war
πολυπραγμονέω: to be busy about many things
φιλόδοξος, -ον: loving honour or glory

εἰ ... ἐστίν: ind. question, "asked *whether he was*"

ὡς δὴ: with the participle πολυπραγμονοῦσα expressing indignation, "why was she busybodying about this?"

ἄλλως ἐπελθόν: aor. part. agreeing with the object of ἤρετο, "she asked (this question) *having approached randomly*" i.e. having come to her for no reason

τὸ πᾶν: acc. adverbial, "completely"

Defective Verbs

The principal parts of some verbs come from completely different words. Sometimes there are more than one form for a specific tense, in which case one will usually be preferred. Here are some important examples:

Present	Future	Aorist	Perfect	Aorist Passive	Translation
ἔρχομαι	εἶμι ἐλεύσομαι	ἦλθον	ἐλήλουθα		to go
φέρω	οἴσω	ἤνεγκα ἤνεγκον	ἐνήνοχα	ἠνέχθην	to bear, carry
λέγω	ἐρέω λέξω	εἶπον ἔλεξα	εἴρηκα λέλεγμαι	ἐρρήθην ἐλέχθην	to speak

ΕΡΜΗΣ: Τὸ μὲν ἀληθὲς οὐκ ἔχω εἰπεῖν, εἰκάζειν δὲ χρὴ νέον ὄντα καὶ τούτων ὀρέγεσθαι τυχεῖν καὶ βούλεσθαι ἂν πρῶτον αὐτὸν εἶναι κατὰ τὰς μάχας.

ΑΦΡΟΔΙΤΗ: Ὁρᾷς, οὐδὲν ἐγὼ μέμφομαι οὐδὲ ἐγκαλῶ σοι τὸ πρὸς ταύτην ἰδίᾳ λαλεῖν· μεμψιμοίρων γὰρ καὶ οὐκ Ἀφροδίτης τὰ τοιαῦτα.

ΕΡΜΗΣ: Καὶ αὕτη σχεδὸν τὰ αὐτά με ἤρετο· διὸ μὴ χαλεπῶς ἔχε μηδ' οἴου μειονεκτεῖν, εἴ τι καὶ ταύτῃ κατὰ τὸ ἁπλοῦν ἀπεκρινάμην. ἀλλὰ μεταξὺ λόγων ἤδη πολὺ προϊόντες

ἀληθής, -ές: unconcealed, true
ἁπλόος, -η, -οῦν: simple
ἀποκρίνομαι: to answer
βούλομαι: to will, wish, be willing
διό: wherefore, on which account
ἐγκαλέω: to reproach
εἰκάζω: to suppose
ἔχω: I am able (+ inf.)
ἴδιος, -α, -ον: one's own, private
λαλέω: to talk
μάχη, ἡ: battle, fight, combat
μειονεκτέω: to have too little, to be poor

μέμφομαι: to blame
μεμψίμοιρος, -ον: repining, querulous
μεταξύ: between (+ gen.)
νέος, -η, -ον: young
οἴομαι: to suppose, think, deem
ὀρέγω: to reach, acquire
προέρχομαι to advance
σχεδόν: close, near
τυγχάνω: to hit
χαλεπός, -ή, -όν: hard to bear
χρή: it is fated, necessary

τὸ ἀληθὲς: acc. adverbial, "truly"
εἰπεῖν: aor. inf. after ἔχω, "able *to say*"
εἰκάζειν: pres. inf. after χρὴ and introducing ind. st., "necessary *to suppose* that ..."
ὄντα: pres. part. causal agreeing with the subject of ὀρέγεσθαι, "suppose that he, *since he is* young, yearns to" + inf.
τυχεῖν: aor. inf. complementing ὀρέγεσθαι, "yearns *to acquire*" + gen.
βούλεσθαι: pres. inf. also in ind. st. after εἰκάζειν, representing a potential optative with ἂν, "suppose *that he would wish to*" + inf.
τὸ ... λαλεῖν: articular inf. serving as object of ἐγκαλῶ, "reproach *the talking* privately"
τὰ τοιαῦτα: acc. of respect, "querulous *about such things*"
μὴ χαλεπῶς ἔχε: imper., "don't keep yourself harshly" i.e. don't be difficult
μηδ' οἴου: imper. mid., "and don't suppose!" + inf.
κατὰ τὸ ἁπλοῦν: "in a simply manner" i.e. without guile
μεταξὺ λόγων: "between words" i.e. while we were speaking
προϊόντες: pres. part., "already *advancing*"

ἀπεσπάσαμεν τῶν ἀστέρων καὶ σχεδόν γε κατὰ τὴν Φρυγίαν ἐσμέν. ἐγὼ δὲ καὶ τὴν Ἴδην ὁρῶ καὶ τὸ Γάργαρον ὅλον ἀκριβῶς, εἰ δὲ μὴ ἐξαπατῶμαι, καὶ αὐτὸν ὑμῶν τὸν δικαστὴν τὸν Πάριν.

ΗΡΑ: Ποῦ δέ ἐστιν; οὐ γὰρ κἀμοὶ φαίνεται.

ΕΡΜΗΣ: Ταύτῃ, ὦ Ἥρα, πρὸς τὰ λαιὰ περισκόπει, μὴ πρὸς ἄκρῳ τῷ ὄρει, παρὰ δὲ τὴν πλευράν, οὗ τὸ ἄντρον, ἔνθα καὶ τὴν ἀγέλην ὁρᾷς.

ἀγέλη, ἡ: a herd
ἀκριβής, -ές: exact, accurate
ἄκρος, -α, -ον: at the furthest point
ἄντρον, τό: cave
ἀποσπάω: to tear or drag away from
ἀστήρ, -έρος, ὁ: a star
δικαστής, -οῦ, ὁ: a judge
ἔνθα: there

ἐξαπατάω: to deceive or beguile
λαιός, -ά, -όν: on the left
ὅλος, -η, -ον: whole, entire
ὄρος, -εος: a mountain, hill
περισκοπέω: to look round
πλευρά, -ᾶς, ἡ: a rib, side
σχεδόν: close, near
φαίνομαι: to appear

τῶν ἀστέρων: gen. after ἀπεσπάσαμεν, "separated *from the stars*"
εἰ δὲ μὴ ἐξαπατῶμαι: pres. in simple protasis, "unless I am mistaken"
κἀμοὶ (=καὶ ἐμοὶ): "appears *also to me*"
περισκόπει: pres. imper., "look around!"
οὗ ... ὁρᾷς: relative clause, "where you see"

Imperatives

There are many more imperatives in Lucian's dialogues, so it is worth reviewing their forms. Here is the regular conjugation of the present and first aorist illustrated with λύω:

Number	Person	Present Imperative		Aorist Imperative		
		Active	*Middle / Passive*	*Active*	*Middle*	*Passive*
Singular	2nd	λῦε	λύου (from ε-σο)	λῦσον	λῦσαι	λύθητι
	3rd	λυέτω	λυέσθω	λυσάτω	λυσάσθω	λυθήτω
Plural	2nd	λύετε	λύεσθε	λύσατε	λύσασθε	λύθητε
	3rd	λυόντων	λυέσθων	λυσάντων	λυσάσθων	λυθέντων

The imperatives of second aorist verbs regularly take the same endings as the present imperative: λαβέ, λαβέτω, etc.

The perfect imperative is rare.

ΗΡΑ: Ἀλλ᾽ οὐχ ὁρῶ τὴν ἀγέλην.

ΕΡΜΗΣ: Πῶς φής; οὐχ ὁρᾷς βοίδια κατὰ τὸν ἐμὸν οὑτωσὶ δάκτυλον ἐκ μέσων τῶν πετρῶν προερχόμενα καί τινα ἐκ τοῦ σκοπέλου καταθέοντα καλαύροπα ἔχοντα καὶ ἀνείργοντα μὴ πρόσω διασκίδνασθαι τὴν ἀγέλην;

ΗΡΑ: Ὁρῶ νῦν, εἴ γε ἐκεῖνός ἐστιν.

ἀγέλη, ἡ: a herd
ἀνείργω: to keep back, restrain
βοίδιον, τό: a cow
δάκτυλος, ὁ: a finger
διασκίδνημι: to scatter
καλαύροψ, -οπος, ἡ: a shepherd's staff

καταθέω: to run down
μέσος, -η, -ον: middle, in the middle
πέτρα, ἡ: a rock, a ledge or shelf of rock
πρόσω: forwards, onwards
σκόπελος, ὁ: a look-out place, a peak

κατὰ ... δάκτυλον: "along my finger" i.e. where I am pointing
προερχόμενα: pres. part. agreeing with βοίδια, "cattle *approaching*"
καταθέοντα: pres. part. agreeing with τινα, "and someone *rushing down*"
μὴ ... διασκίδνασθαι: noun clause after ἀνείργοντα, "keeping the herd *from scattering*"

Circumstantial Participles

Circumstantial participles are added to a noun or a pronoun to set forth some circumstance under which an action takes place. The circumstances can be of the following types: time, manner, means, cause, purpose, concession, condition or attendant circumstance. Although sometimes particles can specify the type of circumstance, often only the context can clarify its force. Here are some examples:

Time: τοῦ δὲ ἀγῶνος τὸ ἆθλον εἴσῃ ἀναγνοὺς τὸ μῆλον: "you will know the prize of the contest *after having read* the apple."

Means: ἵνα μὴ διαταράξωμεν αὐτὸν ἄνωθεν ἐξ ἀφανοῦς καθιπτάμενοι: "lest we frighten him *by flying* suddenly from above"

Purpose: τούτω σοι παραδώσω ἡγεμόνε τῆς ὁδοῦ γενησομένω: "these two I shall hand over *in order to become* leaders of the journey"

Cause: εἰκάζειν δὲ χρὴ νέον ὄντα καὶ τούτων ὀρέγεσθαι τυχεῖν: "One should assume that, *since he is young,* he wishes to acquire these things.".

Condition: δοκῶ δ᾽ ἄν μοι καλῶς δικάσαι πάσαις ἀποδοὺς τὸ μῆλον. "I think that I would judge well, *if I gave* the apple to all."

Attendant Circumstance: οὐχ ὁρᾷς βοίδια κατὰ τὸν ἐμὸν οὑτωσὶ δάκτυλον ἐκ μέσων τῶν πετρῶν προερχόμενα: "do you not see the herd *approaching* from the rocks according to my finger."

The circumstantial participle can also stand in the genitive absolute construction:
ὥστε καὶ πόλεμον ἀμφ᾽ αὐτῇ γενέσθαι, τοῦ Θησέως ἄωρον ἔτι ἁρπάσαντος.: "so that there was a war over her, Theseus *having snatched* her in her youth."

ΕΡΜΗΣ: Ἀλλὰ ἐκεῖνος. ἐπειδὴ δὲ πλησίον ἤδη ἐσμέν, ἐπὶ
τῆς γῆς, εἰ δοκεῖ, καταστάντες βαδίζωμεν, ἵνα μὴ διαταράξωμεν αὐτὸν ἄνωθεν ἐξ ἀφανοῦς καθιπτάμενοι.

ΗΡΑ: Εὖ λέγεις, καὶ οὕτω ποιῶμεν. ἐπεὶ δὲ καταβεβήκαμεν, ὥρα σοι, ὦ Ἀφροδίτη, προϊέναι καὶ ἡγεῖσθαι ἡμῖν
τῆς ὁδοῦ· σὺ γὰρ ὡς τὸ εἰκὸς ἔμπειρος εἶ τοῦ χωρίου
πολλάκις, ὡς λόγος, κατελθοῦσα πρὸς Ἀγχίσην.

ΑΦΡΟΔΙΤΗ: Οὐ σφόδρα, ὦ Ἥρα, τούτοις ἄχθομαι τοῖς
σκώμμασιν.

ΕΡΜΗΣ: Ἀλλ' οὖν ἐγὼ ὑμῖν ἡγήσομαι· καὶ γὰρ αὐτὸς
ἐνδιέτριψα τῇ Ἴδῃ, ὁπότε δὴ ὁ Ζεὺς ἤρα τοῦ μειρακίου

ἄνωθεν: from above, from on high	καταπέτομαι: to fly down
ἀφανής, -ές: unseen, invisible	κατέρχομαι: to go down
ἄχθομαι: to be vexed	μειράκιον, τό: a boy, lad, stripling
βαδίζω: to go slowly, to walk	ὁδός, ἡ: a way, path, track
διαταράττω: to throw into great confusion	πλησίον: near
εἰκός, -ότος, τό: like truth	ποιέω: to make
ἔμπειρος, -ον: experienced in	πολλάκις: many times, often
ἐνδιατρίβω: to spend time in	σκῶμμα, -ατος, τό: a jest, scoff
ἐράω: to love, to be in love with	σφόδρα: very, very much
ἡγέομαι: to go before, lead the way	χωρίον, τό: a particular place
καθίστημι: to set down, place	ὥρα, ἡ: period of time
καταβαίνω: to step down, go or come down	

ἀλλὰ ἐκεῖνος: "*but that* is him"

καταστάντες: aor. part. intransitive, "having set down"

βαδίζωμεν: pres. subj. hortatory, "let us go on foot"

ἵνα μὴ διαταράξωμεν: aor. subj. of δια-ταράττω in negative purpose clause, "lest we
  disturb"

καθιπτάμενοι: pres. part. instrumental of κατα-πέτομαι, "disturb *by flying down*"

καταβεβήκαμεν: perf. of κατα-βαίνω, "when *we have descended*"

προϊέναι καὶ ἡγεῖσθαι: pres. inf. epexegetic after ὥρα, "time *to go ahead and lead*"

ὡς τὸ εἰκός: "as is likely" i.e. apparently

ὡς λόγος: "as the story goes"

Ἀγχίσην: Anchises, a Trojan lover of Aphrodite and father of Aeneas

ἐνδιέτριψα: aor. of ἐν-δια-τρίβω, "I spent time in" + dat.

ἤρα: impf. of ἐράω, "Zeus *used to love*" + gen.

τοῦ Φρυγός, καὶ πολλάκις δεῦρο ἦλθον ὑπ' ἐκείνου καταπεμφθεὶς εἰς ἐπισκοπὴν τοῦ παιδός. καὶ ὁπότε γε ἤδη ἐν τῷ ἀετῷ ἦν, συμπαριπτάμην αὐτῷ καὶ συνεκούφιζον τὸν καλόν, καὶ εἴ γε μέμνημαι, ἀπὸ ταυτησὶ τῆς πέτρας αὐτὸν ἀνήρπασεν. ὁ μὲν γὰρ ἔτυχε τότε

ἀετός, -οῦ, ὁ: an eagle
ἀναρπάζω: to snatch up
δεῦρο: hither
ἐπισκοπή, ἡ: a watching over, visitation
ἔρχομαι: to come or go
καταπέμπω: to send down
μιμνήσκω: to remind, put

παῖς, παιδός, ὁ: a child
πέτρα, ἡ: a rock, a ledge or shelf of rock
πολλάκις: many times, often, oft
συγκουφίζω: to help to lighten
συνπαρίπταμαι: to fly beside with (+ *dat.*)
τότε: at that time, then
τυγχάνω: to happen to (+ *part.*)

Φρυγός: the Phrygian youth is Ganymede
καταπεμφθεὶς: part. aor. pass., "I *having been sent*"
ἐν τῷ ἀετῷ: "when Zeus was *in the eagle*" i.e. when he had taken the form of an eagle
συμπαριπτάμην: impf. of συν-παρα-ἵπταμαι, "I used to fly alongside with" + dat.
μέμνημαι: perf., "if I remember"
ἀπὸ ταυτησὶ: "*from this very* rock"
ἀνήρπασεν: aor. of ἀνα-ἁρπάζω, "he snatched up"

Participles: General Principles

Participles fall into three broad classes of use, with many other distinctions:

1. Attributive participles modify a noun or pronoun like other adjectives. They can occur with an article in the attributive position or with no article:

αἱ νενικημέναι μηδὲ κακὸν ἐντρίψησθε τῷ νεανίσκῳ: "*You who have been defeated* do not harm the lad."

2. Circumstantial participles are added to a noun or pronoun to set forth some circumstance under which an action takes place. Although agreeing with a noun or pronoun, these participles actually qualify the verb in a sentence, indicating time, manner, means, cause, purpose, concession, condition or attendant circumstance. Circumstantial participles can occur in the genitive absolute construction.

καὶ πολλάκις δεῦρο ἦλθον ὑπ' ἐκείνου καταπεμφθεὶς: "I have come here many times, *having been sent* by him"

For more examples, see p. 12

3. Supplementary participles complete the idea of certain verbs. Often it is the participle itself that expresses the main action:

ὁ μὲν γὰρ ἔτυχε τότε συρίζων: "For he happened *to be playing the flute*"

The participial form of indirect discourse after verbs of showing and perceiving is a special class of supplementary participles.

συρίζων πρὸς τὸ ποίμνιον, καταπτάμενος δὲ ὄπισθεν
αὐτοῦ ὁ Ζεὺς κούφως μάλα τοῖς ὄνυξι περιβαλὼν καὶ
τῷ στόματι τὴν ἐπὶ τῇ κεφαλῇ τιάραν ἔχων ἀνέφερε τὸν
παῖδα τεταραγμένον καὶ τῷ τραχήλῳ ἀπεστραμμένῳ εἰς
αὐτὸν ἀποβλέποντα. τότε οὖν ἐγὼ τὴν σύριγγα λαβών,
ἀποβεβλήκει γὰρ αὐτὴν ὑπὸ τοῦ δέους — ἀλλὰ γὰρ ὁ

The Judgment of Paris.
From Attic Red Figure Kylix. (Antikenmuseen, Berlin, Germany.)

ἀναφέρω: to bring or carry up	ὄπισθεν: behind, at the back
ἀποβάλλω: to throw off	παῖς, παιδός, ὁ: a child
ἀποβλέπω: to look toward	περιβάλλω: to throw round, embrace
ἀποστρέφω: to turn back	ποίμνιον, τό: a flock
δέος, δέους, τό: fear, alarm, affright	στόμα, τό: the mouth
καταπέτομαι: to fly down	σῦριγξ, -ιγγος, ἡ: a pipe
κεφαλή, ἡ: the head	συρίζω: to play the σῦριγξ, to pipe
κούφως: delicately	ταράττω: to stir up, trouble
λαμβάνω: to take	τιάρα, ἡ: a tiara
μάλα: very, exceedingly	τότε: at that time, then
ὄνυξ, -υχος, ὁ: a talon	τράχηλος, ὁ: the neck, throat

συρίζων: pres. part. supplementing ἔτυχε, "he happened *to be playing the flute*"

τιάραν: this is the typical Persian head-dress, anachronistically applied to the Phrygian Ganymede

τεταραγμένον: perf. part. of ταράττω, "having been frightened"

ἀπεστραμμένῳ: perf. part. dat. of ἀπο-στρέφω, "with his neck *turned back*"

ἀποβλέποντα: pres. part. acc., "him *looking toward*"

λαβών: aor. part., "I *having taken* his syrinx"

ἀποβεβλήκει: plupf. of ἀπο-βάλλω, "for *he had dropped* it"

15

διαιτητὴς οὑτοσὶ πλησίον, ὥστε προσείπωμεν αὐτόν.
Χαῖρε, ὦ βουκόλε.

ΠΑΡΙΣ: Νὴ καὶ σύ γε, ὦ νεανίσκε. τίς δὲ ὢν δεῦρο ἀφῖξαι
πρὸς ἡμᾶς; ἢ τίνας ταύτας ἄγεις τὰς γυναῖκας; οὐ γὰρ
ἐπιτήδειαι ὀρεοπολεῖν, οὕτως γε οὖσαι καλαί.

ΕΡΜΗΣ: Ἀλλ' οὐ γυναῖκές εἰσιν, Ἥραν δέ, ὦ Πάρι, καὶ
Ἀθηνᾶν καὶ Ἀφροδίτην ὁρᾷς· κἀμὲ τὸν Ἑρμῆν ἀπέστειλεν ὁ Ζεύς — ἀλλὰ τί τρέμεις καὶ ὠχριᾷς; μὴ δέδιθι·
χαλεπὸν γὰρ οὐδέν. κελεύει δέ σε δικαστὴν γενέσθαι τοῦ
κάλλους αὐτῶν· «Ἐπεὶ γάρ,» φησί, «καλός τε αὐτὸς εἶ
καὶ σοφὸς τὰ ἐρωτικά, σοὶ τὴν γνῶσιν ἐπιτρέπω.» τοῦ
δὲ ἀγῶνος τὸ ἆθλον εἴσῃ ἀναγνοὺς τὸ μῆλον.

ἄγω: to lead or carry
ἀγών, -ον, ὁ: a contest
ἆθλον, τό: the prize of contest
ἀναγιγνώσκω: to read
ἀποστέλλω: to send off or away from
ἀφικνέομαι: to come to
γνῶσις, -εως, ἡ: a judicial inquiry
γυνή, γυναικός, ἡ: a woman
δέδια: to fear (*perf.*)
δεῦρο: hither
διαιτητής, -οῦ, ὁ: an arbitrator
δικαστής, -οῦ, ὁ: a judge
ἐπιτήδειος, -α, -ον: suitable, convenient
ἐπιτρέπω: to turn over X (*acc.*) to Y (*dat.*)

ἐρωτικός, -ή, -όν: amatory
κάλλος, -ους, τό: beauty
κελεύω: to command, order
νεανίσκος, ὁ: a young man
νή: indeed
ὀρεοπολέω: to haunt mountains
πλησίον: near
προσεῖπον: to speak to, address
σοφός, -ή, -όν: skilled in any craft
τρέμω: to tremble or fear to
φημί: to declare, make known
χαίρω: to rejoice, be glad
χαλεπός, -ή, -όν: hard to bear, painful
ὠχριάω: to be pallid

ὥστε προσείπωμεν: aor. subj. hortatory, "*and so let's address* him"
ἀφῖξαι: perf., "have you come?"
ὀρεοπολεῖν: pres. inf. epexegetic after ἐπιτήδειαι, "suitable *to haunt mountains*"
οὖσαι: pres. part. causal, "since there are"
ἀπέστειλεν: aor., "he has sent me"
μὴ δέδιθι: perf. imperative, "don't fear!"
γενέσθαι: aor. inf. of γίγνομαι in indirect command, "orders you *to become*"
εἴσῃ: fut. of οἶδα, "you will know"
ἀναγνοὺς: aor. part. of ἀνα-γιγνώσκω, "after having read"

ΠΑΡΙΣ: Φέρ' ἴδω τί καὶ βούλεται. «Ἡ καλή,» φησίν, «λαβέτω.» πῶς ἂν οὖν, ὦ δέσποτα Ἑρμῆ, δυνηθείην ἐγὼ θνητὸς αὐτὸς καὶ ἀγροῖκος ὢν δικαστὴς γενέσθαι παραδόξου θέας καὶ μείζονος ἢ κατὰ βουκόλον; τὰ γὰρ τοιαῦτα κρίνειν τῶν ἀβρῶν μᾶλλον καὶ ἀστικῶν· τὸ δὲ ἐμόν, αἶγα μὲν αἰγὸς ὁποτέρα ἡ καλλίων καὶ δάμαλιν ἄλλης δαμάλεως, τάχ' ἂν δικάσαιμι κατὰ τὴν τέχνην· αὗται δὲ πᾶσαί τε ὁμοίως καλαὶ καὶ οὐκ οἶδ' ὅπως ἄν τις ἀπὸ τῆς ἑτέρας ἐπὶ τὴν ἑτέραν μεταγάγοι τὴν ὄψιν

ἀβρός, -ά, -όν: delicate, beauteous
ἀγροῖκος, -ον: of or in the country
αἴξ, αἰγός, ὁ: a goat
ἀστικός, -ή, -όν: of a city or town
βουκόλος, ὁ: herdsman
βούλομαι: to will, wish, be willing
δάμαλις, -εως, ὁ: a heifer
δεσπότης, -ου: a master
δικάζω: to judge, to give judgment on
δύναμαι: to be able, capable
θέα, ἡ: a seeing, looking at, view
θνητός, -ή, -όν: liable to death, mortal

κρίνω: to judge, choose
μᾶλλον: more, rather
μείζων, -ον: greater
μετάγω: to transfer
ὅμοιος, -α, -ον: like, resembling
ὁπότερος, α, -ον: which of two
ὄψις, ἡ: look, appearance, aspect
παράδοξος, -ον: incredible, paradoxical
πῶς: how? in what way or manner?
τάχα: quickly, presently, forthwith
τέχνη, ἡ: art, skill
φημί: to declare, make known

ἴδω: aor. subj. hortatory., "come, *let me see*"

λαβέτω: aor. 3 s. of λαμβάνω, "let her take!"

πῶς ἂν ... δυνηθείην: aor. pass. opt. potential, "how would I be able" + inf.

δικαστὴς: nom. pred. after γενέσθαι, "become *a judge*" + gen.

κατὰ βουκόλον: after μείζονος ἢ, "greater than *what is related to a herdsman*"

τῶν ἀβρῶν ... ἀστικῶν: gen. after μᾶλλον, "more (suitable for) *dainty and urbane*"

ὁποτέρα: introducing ind. quest. after δικάσαιμι, "judge *which of two* is the more beautiful"

τὸ δὲ ἐμόν: "as for me"

ἂν δικάσαιμι: aor. opt. potential, "I could judge"

ὅπως ἄν τις ... μεταγάγοι: aor. opt. pot. in ind. question after οἶδα, "know *how anyone could transfer*"

τὴν ὄψιν: here "the organs of sight" i.e. the eyes

17

ἀποσπάσας· οὐ γὰρ ἐθέλει ἀφίστασθαι ῥᾳδίως, ἀλλ'
ἔνθα ἂν ἀπερείσῃ τὸ πρῶτον, τούτου ἔχεται καὶ τὸ
παρὸν ἐπαινεῖ· κἂν ἐπ' ἄλλο μεταβῇ, κἀκεῖνο καλὸν ὁρᾷ
καὶ παραμένει, καὶ ὑπὸ τῶν πλησίον παραλαμβάνεται.
καὶ ὅλως περικέχυταί μοι τὸ κάλλος αὐτῶν καὶ ὅλον
περιείληφέ με καὶ ἄχθομαι, ὅτι μὴ καὶ αὐτὸς ὥσπερ ὁ
Ἄργος ὅλῳ βλέπειν δύναμαι τῷ σώματι. δοκῶ δ' ἄν μοι
καλῶς δικάσαι πάσαις ἀποδοὺς τὸ μῆλον. καὶ γὰρ αὖ

ἀπερείδω: to rest, fix, settle
ἀποδίδωμι: to render, award
ἀποσπάω: to tear or drag away from
Ἄργος, ὁ: Argus
αὖ: again, anew
ἀφίστημι: to put away, remove
ἄχθομαι: to be vexed
βλέπω: to see
δικάζω: to judge
δύναμαι: to be able, capable
ἐθέλω: to will, wish, purpose
ἔνθα: there

ἐπαινέω: to approve, praise
κάλλος, -ους, τό: beauty
μεταβαίνω: to pass over from one place to another
ὅλως: completely, altogether
παραλαμβάνω: to distract
παραμένω: to stay near
περιλαμβάνω: embrace
περιχέω: to pour round or over
πλησίον: near
ῥᾴδιος, -α, -ον: easy, ready
σῶμα, σώματος, τό: a body

ἐθέλει: the subject is ὄψις, "the eyes *do not wish*" + inf.
ἂν ἀπερείσῃ: aor. subj. in general locative clause, "wherever they (the eyes) settle"
τούτου: gen. after ἔχεται, "they fix themselves *on this*"
κἂν (=καὶ ἂν) ... μεταβῇ: aor. subj. in present general protasis, "and if ever (the eyes) pass over"
καλὸν: acc. pred., "see that to be *beautiful*"
ὑπὸ τῶν πλησίον: the agency expression, "distracted *by the (things) near*"
περικέχυται: perf. of περι-χέω, "*has been poured around* me"
περιείληφε: perf. of περι-λαμβάνω, " *has embraced* me"
ὁ Ἄργος: "like Argus" the 100-eyed creature set by Hera to watch Io"
ἄν μοι καλῶς δικάσαι: aor. inf. in future less vivid apodosis in ind. st. after δοκῶ, "I think *that I would judge well*"
ἀποδοὺς: aor. part. representing an aor. opt. in a future less vivid protasis, "if I were to award"
καὶ γὰρ αὖ καὶ τόδε: "and moreover this is another thing"

καὶ τόδε, ταύτην μὲν εἶναι συμβέβηκεν τοῦ Διὸς ἀδελφὴν
καὶ γυναῖκα, ταύτας δὲ θυγατέρας: πῶς οὖν οὐ χαλεπὴ
καὶ οὕτως ἡ κρίσις;

ΕΡΜΗΣ: Οὐκ οἶδα: πλὴν οὐχ οἷόν τε ἀναδῦναι πρὸς τοῦ Διὸς
κεκελευσμένον.

ΠΑΡΙΣ: Ἕν τοῦτο, ὦ Ἑρμῆ, πεῖσον αὐτάς, μὴ χαλεπῶς
ἔχειν μοι τὰς δύο τὰς νενικημένας, ἀλλὰ μόνων τῶν
ὀφθαλμῶν ἡγεῖσθαι τὴν διαμαρτίαν.

ΕΡΜΗΣ: Οὕτω φασὶ ποιήσειν: ὥρα δέ σοι ἤδη περαίνειν τὴν
κρίσιν.

ἀδελφή, ἡ: a sister
ἀναδύομαι: to draw back from, shun
διαμαρτία, ἡ: a total mistake
δύο: two
εἷς, μία, ἕν: one
ἡγέομαι: to consider, think
θυγάτηρ, θυγατρός, ἡ: a daughter
κελεύω: to command, order
κρίσις, ἡ: a separating, judgment
μόνος, -η, -ον: alone, only
νικάω: to conquer, prevail, vanquish

ὅδε, ἥδε, τόδε: this
οἷος τε εἰμι: I am able (+ *inf.*)
ὀφθαλμός, ὁ: the eye
πείθω: to prevail upon, persuade
περαίνω: to accomplish, execute
πλήν: but
ποιέω: to make
πῶς: how? in what way or manner?
συμβαίνω: to happen
χαλεπός, -ή, -όν: difficult, painful, grievous
ὥρα, ἡ: period of time, season

ταύτην μὲν ... ταύτας δὲ: acc. subjects of εἶναι, "that *while this one* (Hera) is ... *that these* are"
συμβέβηκεν: perf. of συν-βαίνω used impersonally, "it happens that" + inf.
οὐχ οἷόν τε (sc. ἐστι): "it is not possible" + inf.
κεκελευσμένον: perf. part., "to shun *what is ordered* from Zeus"
πεῖσον: aor. imper. of πείθω, "persuade!"
μὴ χαλεπῶς ἔχειν: ind. com. after πεῖσον, "persuade *not to be angry*"
τὰς νενικημένας: perf. part., "the two *defeated ones*"
ὀφθαλμῶν: gen. pred., "consider the mistake (to be) *of the eyes*"
ποιήσειν: fut. inf., "they say *that they will do*"

19

ΠΑΡΙΣ: Πειρασόμεθα: τί γὰρ ἂν καὶ πάθοι τις; ἐκεῖνο δὲ
πρότερον εἰδέναι βούλομαι, πότερ' ἐξαρκέσει σκοπεῖν αὐτὰς ὡς ἔχουσιν, ἢ καὶ ἀποδῦσαι δεήσει πρὸς τὸ
ἀκριβὲς τῆς ἐξετάσεως;

ΕΡΜΗΣ: Τοῦτο μὲν σὸν ἂν εἴη τοῦ δικαστοῦ, καὶ πρόσταττε
ὅπη καὶ θέλεις.

ΠΑΡΙΣ: Ὅπη καὶ θέλω; γυμνὰς ἰδεῖν βούλομαι.

ΕΡΜΗΣ: Ἀπόδυτε, ὦ αὗται: σὺ δ' ἐπισκόπει: ἐγὼ δὲ
ἀπεστράφην.

ἀκριβής, -ές: exact, accurate
ἀποδύνω: strip off
ἀποστρέφω: to turn away
βούλομαι: to will, wish, be willing
γυμνός, -ή, -όν: naked, unclad
ἐξαρκέω: to suffice for
ἐξέτασις, -εως, ἡ: an examination
ἐπισκοπέω: to inspect, examine
θέλω: to will, wish, purpose

ὅπη: in what way, how (*relative and interrogative adverb*)
πάσχω: to suffer
πειράω: to attempt, endeavour, try
πότερος, -α, -ον: which of the two?
προστάττω: to arrange
πρότερος, -α, -ον: prior
σκοπέω: to look at or after

τί ἂν καὶ πάθοι τις: aor. opt. pot., "what could anyone suffer?" i.e. what can one do?

πότερ' ... ἢ: introducing ind. question in apposition to ἐκεῖνο, "to know this, *namely, whether ... or*"

ἐξαρκέσει ... δεήσει: fut., "it will suffice ... it will be necessary" + inf.

ἂν εἴη: pres. opt. pot., "*this would be* yours"

τοῦ δικαστοῦ: gen. appositive to σὸν according to sense, "your (task), *as judge*"

ἀπεστράφην: aor. pass., "I have turned away"

Potential Optatives

The optative with ἂν expresses potentiality, with a range of possible meanings:

νῦν δὲ ἡδέως ἂν ἀκούσαιμί σου: "I would very much like to hear you"

τί γὰρ ἂν καὶ μωμήσαιτό μου; ""Why would anyone blame me?"

τί γὰρ ἂν καὶ πάθοι τις; "What can one do?"

ΑΦΡΟΔΙΤΗ: Καλῶς, ὦ Πάρι: καὶ πρώτη γε ἀποδύσομαι,
ὅπως μάθῃς ὅτι μὴ μόνας ἔχω τὰς ὠλένας λευκὰς μηδὲ
τῷ βοῶπις εἶναι μέγα φρονῶ, ἐπ' ἴσης δέ εἰμι πᾶσα καὶ
ὁμοίως καλή.

ΑΘΗΝΑ: Μὴ πρότερον ἀποδύσῃς αὐτήν, ὦ Πάρι, πρὶν ἂν
τὸν κεστὸν ἀπόθηται — φαρμακὶς γάρ ἐστιν — μή
σε καταγοητεύσῃ δι' αὐτοῦ. καίτοι γε ἐχρῆν μηδὲ
οὕτω κεκαλλωπισμένην παρεῖναι μηδὲ τοσαῦτα ἐντετριμμένην χρώματα καθάπερ ὡς ἀληθῶς ἑταίραν τινά,
ἀλλὰ γυμνὸν τὸ κάλλος ἐπιδεικνύειν.

ἀποδύνω: strip off
ἀποτίθημι: to put away, stow away
βοῶπις, -ιδος, ἡ: ox-eyed
γυμνός, -ή, -όν: naked, unclad
ἐντρίβω: to rub in or on
ἐπιδείκνυμι: to exhibit, show
ἑταίρα, ἡ: a companion, courtesan
ἴσος, -η, -ον: equal to, the same as
καθάπερ: just as
καίτοι: and indeed, and further
κάλλος, -ους, τό: beauty
καλλωπίζω: to make the face beautiful
καταγοητεύω: to enchant, bewitch

κεστός, ὁ: the girdle of Aphrodite which had magical powers
λευκός, -ή, -όν: light, bright, brilliant
μανθάνω: to learn
μόνος, -η, -ον: alone, left alone
ὅμοιος, -α, -ον: like, resembling
πάρειμι: to be present
πρίν: before
πρότερος, -α, -ον: prior
πρῶτος, -η, -ον: first
φαρμακίς, -ίδος, ἡ: a sorceress, witch
φρονέω: to think
χρῶμα, -ατος, τό: color
ὠλένη, ἡ: the arm

ὅπως μάθῃς: aor. subj. pass. in purpose clause, "so that you know"

μὴ μόνας ... λευκὰς: "not just white arms" a Homeric expression used for Hera and other goddesses

τῷ βοῶπις: dat. of cause, "because of my 'ox-eyes'" another epithet of Hera

μὴ ... ἀποδύσῃς: aor. subj. in prohibition, "don't undress her!"

πρότερον ... πρὶν: "first ... before"

πρὶν ἂν ... ἀπόθηται: aor. subj. of ἀπο-τίθημι in general temporal clause, "before she sets aside (whenever that is)"

μή ... καταγοητεύσῃ: aor. subj. in neg. jussive clause, "*let her not beguile* you"

ἐχρῆν: the imperfect expresses what should be but is not, "*it ought*" + acc. + inf., i.e. *she should* not be present

κεκαλλωπισμένην ... ἐντετριμμένην: perf. part. circum. agreeing with the subject of παρεῖναι, "after having been beautified ... after having rubbed in"

ἐπιδεικνύειν: pres. inf. also after ἐχρῆν, "she should *show* her beauty"

21

ΠΑΡΙΣ: Εὖ λέγουσι τὸ περὶ τοῦ κεστοῦ, καὶ ἀπόθου.

ΑΦΡΟΔΙΤΗ: Τί οὖν οὐχὶ καὶ σύ, ὦ Ἀθηνᾶ, τὴν κόρυν ἀφελοῦσα ψιλὴν τὴν κεφαλὴν ἐπιδεικνύεις, ἀλλ' ἐπισείεις
τὸν λόφον καὶ τὸν δικαστὴν φοβεῖς; ἢ δέδιας μή σοι
ἐλέγχηται τὸ γλαυκὸν τῶν ὀμμάτων ἄνευ τοῦ φοβεροῦ
βλεπόμενον;

ΑΘΗΝΑ: Ἰδού σοι ἡ κόρυς αὕτη ἀφήρηται.

ΑΦΡΟΔΙΤΗ: Ἰδοὺ καί σοι ὁ κεστός.

ΗΡΑ: Ἀλλὰ ἀποδυσώμεθα.

ΠΑΡΙΣ: Ὦ Ζεῦ τεράστιε τῆς θέας, τοῦ κάλλους, τῆς ἡδονῆς.
οἵα μὲν ἡ παρθένος, ὡς δὲ βασιλικὸν αὕτη καὶ σεμνὸν

ἄνευ: without
ἀποδύνω: strip off
ἀποτίθημι: to put away, stow away
ἀφαιρέω: to take from
βασιλικός, -ή, -όν: royal, kingly
βλέπω: to see
γλαυκός, -ή, -όν: grey
δέδια: to fear (perf.)
ἐλέγχω: to disgrace, put to shame
ἐπιδεικνύω: to show
ἐπισείω: to shake at or against
θέα, ἡ: a seeing, sight
κάλλος, -ους, τό: beauty

κεστός, ὁ: the girdle of Aphrodite
κεφαλή, ἡ: the head
κόρυς, ἡ: a helmet
λόφος, ὁ: the crest (of a helmet)
οἷος, -ά, -όν: what sort?
ὄμμα, -ατος, τό: an eye
παρθένος, ἡ: a maid, virgin
σεμνός, -ή, -όν: revered, august
τεράστιος, -ον: monstrous
φοβερός, -ά, -όν: fearful
φοβέω: to put to flight
ψιλός, -ή, -όν: bare

ἀπόθου: aor. imper. of ἀπο-τίθημι, "take off!"

ἀφελοῦσα: aor. part. of ἀπο-αἱρέω, "having removed"

ψιλὴν: acc. pred., "show your head *bare*"

μή ... ἐλέγχηται: pres. subj. after verb of fearing, "fear *that it will disgrace*"

τὸ γλαυκὸν: "the grey" of Athena's eyes was a standard part of her description in
 Homer, but by Lucian's time the word was not complimentary. See Pötscher.

ἀφήρηται: perf. of ἀπο-αἱρέω, "it has been removed"

ἀποδυσώμεθα: aor. subj. hortatory, "let us undress"

τῆς θέας, etc.: gen. of exclamation, "what a sight! what beauty!"

ὡς ... βασιλικὸν ... σεμνὸν ... ἄξιον: acc. adverbial, "how *royally and holy and worthily*
 she shines"

ἀπολάμπει καὶ ἀληθῶς ἄξιον τοῦ Διός, ἥδε δὲ ὁρᾷ ἡδύ
τι καὶ γλαφυρόν, καὶ προσαγωγὸν ἐμειδίασεν — ἀλλ'
ἤδη μὲν ἅλις ἔχω τῆς εὐδαιμονίας: εἰ δοκεῖ δέ, καὶ ἰδίᾳ
καθ' ἑκάστην ἐπιδεῖν βούλομαι, ὡς νῦν γε ἀμφίβολός
εἰμι καὶ οὐκ οἶδα πρὸς ὅ τι ἀποβλέψω, πάντῃ τὰς ὄψεις
περισπώμενος.

ΑΦΡΟΔΙΤΗ: Οὕτω ποιῶμεν.

ΠΑΡΙΣ: Ἄπιτε οὖν αἱ δύο: σὺ δέ, ὦ Ἥρα, περίμενε.

ΗΡΑ: Περιμενῶ, κἀπειδάν με ἀκριβῶς ἴδῃς, ὥρα σοι καὶ
τἄλλα ἤδη σκοπεῖν εἰ καλά σοι, τὰ δῶρα τῆς ψήφου τῆς
ἐμῆς. ἢν γάρ με, ὦ Πάρι, δικάσῃς εἶναι καλήν, ἁπάσης
ἔσῃ τῆς Ἀσίας δεσπότης.

ἀκριβής, -ές: exact, accurate
ἅλις: in abundance, in plenty
ἀμφίβολος, -ον: doubtful
ἄξιος, -α, -ον: worthy of
ἀποβλέπω: to look away towards
ἀπολάμπω: to shine or beam from
Ἀσία, ἡ: Asia
βούλομαι: to will, wish
γλαφυρός, -ά, -όν: delicate
δεσπότης, -ου: a master, lord
δικάζω: to judge
δῶρον, τό: a gift, present
ἕκαστος, -η, -ον: every, each
ἐπειδάν: whenever + subj.
ἐπεῖδον: (aor.) to look upon, behold

εὐδαιμονία, ἡ: prosperity, happiness
ἡδονή, ἡ: pleasure
ἡδύς, -εῖα, -υ: sweet
ἴδιος, -α, -ον: one's own
μειδιάω: to smile
ὄψις, ἡ: look, appearance, aspect
πάντῃ: every way, on every side
περιμένω: to wait for, stay
περισπάω: to draw away from
ποιέω: to make
προσαγωγός, -όν: attractive
σκοπέω: to look at
ψῆφος, ἡ: a pebble for voting, a vote
ὥρα, ἡ: period of time

ἡδύ ... γλαφυρόν: acc. adverbial, "sweetly and refined"

ἐπιδεῖν: aor. inf. after βούλομαι, "wish *to look upon*"

ὅ τι ἀποβλέψω: aor. subj. in ind. deliberative question, "know *what I should look at*"

περισπώμενος: pres. part. mid., "*diverting* my eyes"

ποιῶμεν: subj. hortatory, "*let us do so*"

ἄπιτε: imper., "go away!"

κἀπειδάν ... ἴδῃς: aor. subj. in general temporal clause, "and when(ever) you see me"

ἢν ... δικάσῃς: aor. subj. in future more vivid protasis, "if you judge"

καλήν: acc. pred., "judge me to be *beautiful*"

ἔσῃ: fut. in more vivid apodosis, "then you will be"

ΠΑΡΙΣ: Οὐκ ἐπὶ δώροις μὲν τὰ ἡμέτερα. πλὴν ἄπιθι:
πεπράξεται γὰρ ἅπερ ἂν δοκῇ. σὺ δὲ πρόσιθι ἡ Ἀθηνᾶ.

ΑΘΗΝΑ: Παρέστηκά σοι, καὶ ἢν με, ὦ Πάρι, δικάσῃς καλήν,
οὔποτε ἥττων ἄπει ἐκ μάχης, ἀλλ᾽ ἀεὶ κρατῶν: πολε-
μιστὴν γάρ σε καὶ νικηφόρον ἀπεργάσομαι.

ἀεί: always, for ever
ἀπεργάζομαι: to cause to turn out
δικάζω: to judge
δῶρον, τό: a gift, present
ἡμέτερος, -α, -ον: our
ἤν: if (+ *subj.*)
ἥττων, -ον: inferior
κρατέω: to be strong, mighty

μάχη, ἡ: battle, fight, combat
νικηφόρος, -ον: victorious
παρίστημι: to make to stand beside
πλήν: but
πολεμιστής, -οῦ, ὁ: a warrior
πράττω: to do
πρόσειμι: to approach

πεπράξεται: fut. perf., "will have been done"

ἅπερ ἂν δοκῇ: pres. subj. in general relative clause, serving as the subject of πεπράξεται, "what(ever) seems right"

πρόσιθι: aor. imper., "approach!"

παρέστηκα: perf. of παρα-ίστημι, "I have stood up alongside" i.e. I am standing next to" + dat.

ἢν (= εἰ ἄν) ... δικάσῃς: aor. subj. in future more vivid protasis, "if you judge"

ἄπει: fut. of ἀπο-έρχομαι, "then you will depart"

νικηφόρον: acc. pred., "cause you to be *victorious*"

General or Indefinite Clauses

Various kinds of subordinate clauses that are general or indefinite (if ever, whenever, whoever, etc.) use the subjunctive with ἄν in primary sequence, the optative without ἄν in secondary sequence:

μὴ πρότερον ἀποδύσῃς αὐτήν, ὦ Πάρι, πρὶν ἂν τὸν κεστὸν ἀπόθηται: "Do not undress her, Paris, *until such time as she removes* her girdle."

πεπράξεται γὰρ ἅπερ ἂν δοκῇ: "*whatever seems appropriate* will be done"

κἂν ἐπ᾽ ἄλλο μεταβῇ, κἀκεῖνο καλὸν ὁρᾷ καὶ παραμένει: "*if ever (the eyes) pass over* to something else, they see that beauty and remain."

Lucian sometimes uses the optative in the protasis of a present general condition:

ἐκείνη γὰρ εἰ καὶ μόνον θεάσαιτό σε, εὖ οἶδα ἐγὼ ὡς ... ἕψεται καὶ συνοικήσει: "for *if ever she just sees* you, I know that she will follow and live with you.

ΠΑΡΙΣ: Οὐδέν, ὦ Ἀθηνᾶ, δεῖ μοι πολέμου καὶ μάχης· εἰρήνη
γάρ, ὡς ὁρᾷς, τὰ νῦν ἐπέχει τὴν Φρυγίαν τε καὶ Λυδίαν
καὶ ἀπολέμητος ἡμῖν ἡ τοῦ πατρὸς ἀρχή. θάρρει δέ· οὐ
μειονεκτήσεις γάρ, κἂν μὴ ἐπὶ δώροις δικάζωμεν. ἀλλ᾽
ἔνδυθι ἤδη καὶ ἐπίθου τὴν κόρυν· ἱκανῶς γὰρ εἶδον. τὴν
Ἀφροδίτην παρεῖναι καιρός.

ΑΦΡΟΔΙΤΗ: Αὕτη σοι ἐγὼ πλησίον, καὶ σκόπει καθ᾽ ἓν
ἀκριβῶς μηδὲν παρατρέχων, ἀλλ᾽ ἐνδιατρίβων ἑκάστῳ
τῶν μερῶν. εἰ δ᾽ ἐθέλεις, ὦ καλέ, καὶ τάδε μου ἄκουσον.
ἐγὼ γὰρ πάλαι ὁρῶσά σε νέον ὄντα καὶ καλὸν ὁποῖον οὐκ
οἶδα εἴ τινα ἕτερον ἡ Φρυγία τρέφει, μακαρίζω μὲν τοῦ

ἀκούω: to hear
ἀκριβής, -ές: exact, accurate
ἀπολέμητος, -ον: not warred on
ἀρχή, ἡ: an empire, kindgom
δῶρον, τό: a gift, present
ἐθέλω: to will, wish
εἰρήνη, ἡ: peace, time of peace
ἕκαστος, -η, -ον: every, each
ἐνδιατρίβω: to spend time on (+ *dat.*)
ἐνδύνω: to dress, put on clothes
ἐπέχω: to have a hold on
ἐπιτίθημι: to put upon
θαρρέω: to be of good courage
ἱκανός: becoming, sufficing
καιρός, ὁ: the proper time
κόρυς, ἡ: a helmet
Λυδία, ἡ: Lydia

μακαρίζω: to bless, congratulate X (*acc.*) for Y (*gen.*)
μάχη, ἡ: battle, fight, combat
μειονεκτέω: to have too little, to fail
μέρος, -εος, τό: a part
νέος, -η, -ον: new, young
ὁποῖος: of what sort or quality
πάλαι: long ago
παρατρέχω: to run by or past
πάρειμι: to be present
πατήρ, ὁ: a father
πλησίον: near
πόλεμος, ὁ: battle, fight, war
σκοπέω: to look at
τρέφω: to nurture
Φρυγία, ἡ: Phyrgia

τὰ νῦν: acc. adverbial, "at the present time" an oblique reference to the impending Trojan War prompted by this judgment

οὐ μειονεκτήσεις: fut., "you will not fall short"

κἂν ... δικάζωμεν: pres. subj. in future more vivid protasis, "even if we judge"

ἔνδυθι: aor. imperative, "put on your clothes!"

ἐπίθου: aor. imper., "*put on* your helmet!"

παρεῖναι: pres. inf. epexegetic after καιρός, "time *to be present*"

ἄκουσον: aor. imper., "listen to!' + gen.

ὄντα: pres. part. in ind. st. after ὁρῶσά, "seeing *that you are* young"

εἰ ... τρέφει: ind. question, "know *whether Phrygia nourishes*"

κάλλους, αἰτιῶμαι δὲ τὸ μὴ ἀπολιπόντα τοὺς σκοπέλους
καὶ ταυτασὶ τὰς πέτρας κατ' ἄστυ ζῆν, ἀλλὰ διαφθείρειν
τὸ κάλλος ἐν ἐρημίᾳ. τί μὲν γὰρ ἂν σὺ ἀπολαύσειας τῶν
ὀρῶν; τί δ' ἂν ἀπόναιντο τοῦ σοῦ κάλλους αἱ βόες; ἔπρεπεν δὲ ἤδη σοι καὶ γεγαμηκέναι, μὴ μέντοι ἀγροῖκόν τινα
καὶ χωρῖτιν, οἷαι κατὰ τὴν Ἴδην αἱ γυναῖκες, ἀλλά τινα
ἐκ τῆς Ἑλλάδος, ἢ Ἀργόθεν ἢ ἐκ Κορίνθου ἢ Λάκαιναν
οἷάπερ ἡ Ἑλένη ἐστίν, νέα τε καὶ καλὴ καὶ κατ' οὐδὲν
ἐλάττων ἐμοῦ, καὶ τὸ δὴ μέγιστον, ἐρωτική. ἐκείνη γὰρ

ἀγροῖκος, -ον: of or in the country
αἰτιάομαι: to charge, blame
ἀπολαύω: to have enjoyment of
ἀπολείπω: to leave behind
ἀπονίναμαι: to have the use or enjoyment of
Ἀργόθεν: from Argos
ἄστυ, -εως, τό: a city, town
βοῦς, ἡ: a cow
γαμέω: to marry
γυνή, γυναικός, ἡ: a woman
διαφθείρω: to destroy utterly
ἐλάττων, -ον: inferior to (+ gen.)
Ἑλένη, ἡ: Helen
Ἑλλάς, -δος, ἡ: Greece

ἐρημία, ἡ: a desert, wilderness
ἐρωτικός, -ή, -όν: amatory
ζάω: to live
κάλλος, -ους, τό: beauty
Κόρινθος, ὁ: Corinth
Λάκαινα, ἡ: a Laconian woman
μέντοι: indeed
νέος, -η, -ον: new, young
οἷος, -α, -ον: what sort?
ὄρος, -εος, τό: a mountain
πέτρα, ἡ: a rock
πρέπω: to be clearly seen, to be fitting
σκόπελος, ὁ: a peak, promontory
χωρῖτις, -ιδος, ἡ: a rustic, boor

τὸ μὴ ... ζῆν: articular inf. object of αἰτιῶμαι, "I blame the (i.e. your) not living"
ἀπολιπόντα: aor. part. agreeing with the acc. subject of ζῆν, "(you) having left behind"
(τὸ) διαφθείρειν: also articular inf. after αἰτιῶμαι, "but the (i.e. your) wasting"
τί ἂν ἀπολαύσειας: aor. opt. pot., "what benefit could you have?"
ἂν ἀπόναιντο: aor. opt. pot. of ἀπο-ονίναμαι, "why should cows enjoy?" + gen.
ἔπρεπεν: impf. with contrafactual force, "it would be more fitting" + inf.
γεγαμηκέναι: perf. inf. complementing ἔπρεπεν, "fitting to have married"
καὶ τὸ δὴ: "and even more importantly"

εἰ καὶ μόνον θεάσαιτό σε, εὖ οἶδα ἐγὼ ὡς ἅπαντα ἀπολιποῦσα καὶ παρασχοῦσα ἑαυτὴν ἔκδοτον ἕψεται καὶ
συνοικήσει. πάντως δὲ καὶ σὺ ἀκήκοάς τι περὶ αὐτῆς.

ΠΑΡΙΣ: Οὐδέν, ὦ Ἀφροδίτη· νῦν δὲ ἡδέως ἂν ἀκούσαιμί σου
τὰ πάντα διηγουμένης.

ΑΦΡΟΔΙΤΗ: Αὕτη θυγάτηρ μέν ἐστι Λήδας ἐκείνης τῆς
καλῆς ἐφ᾽ ἣν ὁ Ζεὺς κατέπτη κύκνος γενόμενος.

ἀκούω: to hear, listen to (+ *gen.*)
ἀπολείπω: to leave behind, abandon
γίγνομαι: to happen, become
διηγέομαι: to describe in full
ἔκδοτος, -ον: given over
ἕπομαι: to follow
ἡδέως: sweetly
θεάομαι: to look on, gaze at

θυγάτηρ, θυγατρός, ἡ: a daughter
καταπέτομαι: to fly down
κύκνος, ὁ: a swan
Λήδα, -δας, ἡ: Leda
πάντως: completely
παρέχω: to provide, supply
συνοικέω: to live with

εἰ ... θεάσαιτο: aor. opt. in present general protasis, "*if she ever looks upon* you"

ὡς ... ἕψεται καὶ συνοικήσει: fut. in future more vivid apodosis in ind. st. after οἶδα, "I know *that she will follow and live with*"

ἀπολιποῦσα καὶ παρασχοῦσα: aor. part. agreeing with the subject of ἕψεται, "that she, *having abandoned and having delivered* herself"

ἔκδοτον: acc. pred., "delivered herself *as given over*" i.e. in marriage

πάντως: expressing strong affirmation, "*surely* you have heard"

ἀκήκοας: perf., "*you have heard* something"

ἂν ἀκούσαιμι: aor. opt. pot., "I would like to listen to" + gen.

ἐκείνης: "daughter *of that famous* Leda"

κατέπτη: aor. of κατα-πέτομαι, "upon whom Zeus *flew down*"

Translating Participles

Greek has many more participles than English. The aorist participle is quite common and has no parallel in English in most cases. Because English has no way to indicate simple time with a participle, our "translationese" versions of aorist participles will often sound like perfect participles:

εὖ οἶδα ἐγὼ ὡς ἅπαντα ἀπολιποῦσα καὶ παρασχοῦσα ἑαυτὴν ἔκδοτον ἕψεται: "I know well that, *having left* everything and *having given* herself, she will follow you."

More idiomatic in these cases would be some kind of periphrasis, such as "I know that she will leave everything, give herself entirely and follow you," but our translationese version will indicate the syntactic relations more clearly.

27

ΠΑΡΙΣ: Ποία δὲ τὴν ὄψιν ἐστί;

ΑΦΡΟΔΙΤΗ: Λευκὴ μέν, οἵαν εἰκὸς ἐκ κύκνου γεγενημένην, ἀπαλὴ δέ, ὡς ἐν ᾠῷ τραφεῖσα, γυμνὰς τὰ πολλὰ καὶ παλαιστική, καὶ οὕτω δή τι περισπούδαστος ὥστε καὶ πόλεμον ἀμφ' αὐτῇ γενέσθαι, τοῦ Θησέως ἄωρον ἔτι ἁρπάσαντος. οὐ μὴν ἀλλ' ἐπειδήπερ εἰς ἀκμὴν κατέστη, πάντες οἱ ἄριστοι τῶν Ἀχαιῶν ἐπὶ τὴν μνηστείαν ἀπήντησαν, προεκρίθη δὲ Μενέλεως τοῦ Πελοπιδῶν γένους. εἰ δὴ θέλοις, ἐγώ σοι καταπράξομαι τὸν γάμον.

ἀκμή, ἡ: a peak, highest point	καταπράττω: to accomplish, arrange
ἀπαλός, -ή, -όν: soft to the touch, tender	λευκός, -ή, -όν: white, bright
ἀπαντάω: to contend	Μενέλαος, ὁ: Menelaus
ἄριστος, -η, -ον: best	μνηστεία, ἡ: a wooing, courting
ἁρπάζω: to snatch away, carry off	οἷος, -α, -ον: what sort or manner
Ἀχαιός, ὁ: an Achaian	ὄψις, ἡ: look, appearance, aspect
ἄωρον, -ον: unseasonable, unripe	παλαιστικός, -ή, -όν: expert in wrestling
γάμος, ὁ: a wedding	Πελοπίδης, -ου, ὁ: a descendant of Pelops
γένος, -ους, τό: race, stock, family	περισπούδαστος, -ον: much sought after, much desired
γυμνός, -ή, -όν: naked, trained	
εἰκός, τό: probable, likely	ποῖος, -α, -ον: of what sort?
ἐπειδήπερ: after, when	πόλεμος, ὁ: battle, fight, war
θέλω: to will, wish, purpose	προκρίνω: to prefer, select (+ gen.)
Θησεύς, ὁ: Theseus	τρέφω: to nourish
καθίστημι: to set down, establish	ᾠόν, τό: an egg

τὴν ὄψιν: acc. of respect, "what is she *in appearance?*"

οἵαν ... γεγεμένην: perf. part. of γίγνομαι, "as is probable for someone *born from* a swan," the form Zeus took when assaulting the mother of Helen

ὡς ... τραφεῖσα: aor. part. pass. causal, "*since she was nourished* in an egg"

τὰ πολλά: acc. of respect with γυμνάς, "trained *in many things*"

οὕτω δή: "for this very reason"

γενέσθαι: aor. inf. in result clause, "so that a war *happened*"

τοῦ Θησέως ... ἁρπάσαντος: aor. part. in gen. abs., "Theseus having kidnapped her" this abduction occurred while Helen was still a child

οὐ μὴν ἀλλά: indicating a climax, "moreover"

κατέστη: aor. intransitive of κατα-ἵστημι, "when *she arrived* to her maturity"

ἀπήντησαν: aor. of ἀπο-αντάω, "they contended"

προεκρίθη: aor. pass. of προ-κρίνω, "Menelaus *was selected*"

θέλοις: pres. opt. in future less vivid protasis, "if you should wish"

καταπράξομαι: fut. in future more vivid apodosis, "I will arrange"

ΠΑΡΙΣ: Πῶς φής; τὸν τῆς γεγαμημένης;

ΑΦΡΟΔΙΤΗ: Νέος εἶ σὺ καὶ ἀγροῖκος, ἐγὼ δὲ οἶδα ὡς χρὴ τὰ τοιαῦτα δρᾶν.

ΠΑΡΙΣ: Πῶς; ἐθέλω γὰρ καὶ αὐτὸς εἰδέναι.

ΑΦΡΟΔΙΤΗ: Σὺ μὲν ἀποδημήσεις ὡς ἐπὶ θέαν τῆς Ἑλλάδος, κἀπειδὰν ἀφίκῃ εἰς τὴν Λακεδαίμονα, ὄψεταί σε ἡ Ἑλένη. τοὐντεῦθεν δὲ ἐμὸν ἂν εἴη τὸ ἔργον, ὅπως ἐρασθήσεταί σου καὶ ἀκολουθήσει.

ΠΑΡΙΣ: Τοῦτο αὐτὸ καὶ ἄπιστον εἶναί μοι δοκεῖ, τὸ ἀπολιποῦσαν τὸν ἄνδρα ἐθελῆσαι βαρβάρῳ καὶ ξένῳ συνεκπλεῦσαι.

ἀκολουθέω: to follow
ἀνήρ, ἀνδρός, ὁ: an man
ἄπιστος, -ον: incredible
ἀποδημέω: to travel from home
ἀπολείπω: to leave behind
ἀφικνέομαι: to come to, arrive
βάρβαρος, -ον: barbarous
γαμέω: to marry
δράω: to do
ἐθέλω: to will, wish, purpose
Ἑλλάς, -δος, ἡ: Greece

ἐντεῦθεν: hence or thence
ἐπειδάν: whenever + subj.
ἔραμαι: to love, to be in love with
θέα, ἡ: a seeing, looking at, view
Λακεδαίμων, -ονος, ἡ: Lacedaemon
νέος, -η, -ον: young
ξένος, -η, -ον: foreign
συνεκπλέω: to sail out along with
τοιοῦτος, -αύτη, -οῦτο: such as this
χρή: it is fated, necessary

γεγαμημένης: perf. part. of γαμέω, "the (marriage) *of one having been married?*"
ὡς ἐπὶ θέαν: "as though in order to see" i.e. on the pretext of seeing
κἀπειδὰν ἀφίκῃ: aor. subj. in future temporal clause, "when you arrive" i.e. whenever that is
ὄψεται: fut., "Helen *will see*"
τοὐντεῦθεν (=τό ἐντεῦθεν): "from that point"
ἂν εἴη: pres. opt. pot., "the work *would be* mine"
ὅπως ἐρασθήσεται: fut. pass. in noun clause after a verb of effort, "my work would be *to see to it that she falls in love*"
τοῦτο αὐτὸ: emphatic, "this very thing"
τὸ ... ἐθελῆσαι: aor. inf. articular in apposition to τοῦτο, "this, *the her being willing*"
ἀπολιποῦσαν: aor. part. agreeing with the acc. subject of ἐθελῆσαι, "her *having left* her husband"
συνεκπλεῦσαι: aor. inf. complementing ἐθελῆσαι, "wishing *to sail away with*" + dat.

ΑΦΡΟΔΙΤΗ: Θάρρει τούτου γε ἕνεκα. παῖδε γάρ μοι ἐστὸν
δύο καλώ, Ἵμερος καὶ Ἔρως, τούτω σοι παραδώσω
ἡγεμόνε τῆς ὁδοῦ γενησομένω: καὶ ὁ μὲν Ἔρως ὅλος
παρελθὼν εἰς αὐτὴν ἀναγκάσει τὴν γυναῖκα ἐρᾶν, ὁ δ'
Ἵμερος αὐτῷ σοι περιχυθεὶς τοῦθ' ὅπερ ἐστίν, ἱμερτόν
τε θήσει καὶ ἐράσμιον. καὶ αὐτὴ δὲ συμπαροῦσα δεήσομαι καὶ τῶν Χαρίτων ἀκολουθεῖν: καὶ οὕτως ἅπαντες
αὐτὴν ἀναπείσομεν.

ΠΑΡΙΣ: Ὅπως μὲν ταῦτα χωρήσει, ἄδηλον, ὦ Ἀφροδίτη:
πλὴν ἐρῶ γε ἤδη τῆς Ἑλένης καὶ οὐκ οἶδ' ὅπως καὶ ὁρᾶν

ἄδηλος, -ον: unclear
ἀκολουθέω: to follow
ἀναγκάζω: to force, compel
ἀναπείθω: to bring over, convince
δέομαι: to ask (+ *gen.*)
ἕνεκα: on account of (+ *gen.*)
ἐράσμιος, -η, -ον: lovely
ἐράω: to love (+ *gen.*)
Ἔρως, -τος, ὁ: Love
ἡγεμών, -όνος, ἡ: a leader
Ἵμερος, ὁ: Desire

ἱμερτός, -ή, -όν: longed for, lovely
ὁδός, ἡ: a way, path
οἴομαι: to suppose (+ *inf.*)
ὅλος, -η, -ον: whole, entire
παραδίδωμι: to give over
παρέρχομαι: to go beside
περιχέω: to pour X (*acc.*) over Y (*dat.*)
πλήν: but
συμπάρειμι: to go beside together
τίθημι: to set, put, place
χωρέω: to take place

παῖδε ... καλώ: dual, "two beautiful children"
ἐστὸν: pres. 3 person dual, "*there are* two"
τούτω ... ἡγεμόνε: dual, "these two ... leaders"
γενησομένω: fut. part. dual, expressing purpose, "*in order to become* leaders"
παρελθὼν: aor. part., "having come along"
ἐρᾶν: pres. inf. after ἀναγκάσει, "will compell her *to love*"
περιχυθεὶς: aor. part. pass. of περι-χέω, "having poured over"
τοῦθ' ὅπερ ἐστίν: "having poured *this very thing which he is*" i.e. desire
θήσει: fut. of τίθημι, "*he will make* you"
δεήσομαι: fut. of δέομαι, "I will ask" + inf.
ἀναπείσομεν: fut. of ἀνα-πείθω, "we will persuade"
ὅπως ... χωρήσει: fut. in ind. question after ἄδηλον, "unclear *how these will happen*"
οὐκ οἶδ' ὅπως: parenthetical, "I don't know how"
ὁρᾶν: pres. inf. in ind. st. after οἴομαι, "I seem *to see* her"

30

αὐτὴν οἴομαι καὶ πλέω εὐθὺ τῆς Ἑλλάδος καὶ τῇ Σπάρτῃ ἐπιδημῶ καὶ ἐπάνειμι ἔχων τὴν γυναῖκα — καὶ ἄχθομαι ὅτι μὴ ταῦτα ἤδη πάντα ποιῶ.

ΑΦΡΟΔΙΤΗ: Μὴ πρότερον ἐρασθῇς, ὦ Πάρι, πρὶν ἐμὲ τὴν προμνήστριαν καὶ νυμφαγωγὸν ἀμείψασθαι τῇ κρίσει· πρέποι γὰρ ἂν κἀμὲ νικηφόρον ὑμῖν συμπαρεῖναι καὶ ἑορτάζειν ἅμα καὶ τοὺς γάμους καὶ τὰ ἐπινίκια. πάντα γὰρ ἔνεστί σοι — τὸν ἔρωτα, τὸ κάλλος, τὸν γάμον — τουτουὶ τοῦ μήλου πρίασθαι.

ΠΑΡΙΣ: Δέδοικα μή μου ἀμελήσῃς μετὰ τὴν κρίσιν.

ΑΦΡΟΔΙΤΗ: Βούλει οὖν ἐπομόσομαι;

ἀμείβω: to exchange, pay back
ἀμελέω: to have no care for (+ *gen.*)
ἄχθομαι: to be vexed
γάμος, ὁ: a wedding, wedding-feast
δέδοικα: to fear
Ἑλλάς, ἡ: Hellas
ἔνειμι: to be in
ἑορτάζω: to celebrate
ἐπανέρχομαι: to return
ἐπιδημέω: to travel in
ἐπινίκιος, -ον: of victory, triumphal
ἐπόμνυμι: to swear upon
ἔραμαι: to love, to be in love with
εὐθύ: straight towards (+ *gen.*)

κάλλος, -ους, τό: beauty
κρίσις, ἡ: a judgment, decision
μῆλον, τό: apple
νικηφόρος, -ον: victorious
νυμφαγωγός, -όν: leader of the bride
οἴομαι: to suppose, think
πλέω: to sail
πρέπω: to be proper
πρίαμαι: to buy
πρίν: before (+ *inf.*)
προμνήστρια, ἡ: a match-maker
πρότερον: prior
Σπάρτη, ἡ: Sparta
συμπάρειμι: to be with

ἐπάνειμι: fut. of ἐπι-ανα-έρχομαι, "I will return"
ὅτι μὴ ... ποιῶ: noun clause after ἄχθομαι, "vexed *that I am not doing*"
μὴ ... ἐρασθῇς: aor. subj. pass. in prohibition, "don't become enamoured!"
ἀμείψασθαι: aor. inf. mid. after πρὶν, "before *having requited* me"
τῇ κρίσει: dat. means, "requited *with your decision*"
πρέποι: pres. opt. pot., "it would be proper" + inf.
τοῦ μήλου: gen. of value, "buy *for this apple*"
πρίασθαι: aor. inf. complementing ἔνεστι: "it is in your power *to buy*"
μὴ μου ἀμελήσῃς: aor. subj. after verb of fearing, "I fear *you will not care*"
ἐπομόσομαι: fut. after βούλει, "do you wish *that I swear?*"

ΠΑΡΙΣ: Μηδαμῶς, ἀλλ' ὑπόσχου πάλιν.

ΑΦΡΟΔΙΤΗ: Ὑπισχνοῦμαι δή σοι τὴν Ἑλένην παραδώσειν γυναῖκα, καὶ ἀκολουθήσειν γέ σοι αὐτὴν καὶ ἀφίξεσθαι παρ' ὑμᾶς εἰς τὴν Ἴλιον: καὶ αὐτὴ παρέσομαι καὶ συμπράξω τὰ πάντα.

ΠΑΡΙΣ: Καὶ τὸν Ἔρωτα καὶ τὸν Ἴμερον καὶ τὰς Χάριτας ἄξεις;

ΑΦΡΟΔΙΤΗ: Θάρρει, καὶ τὸν Πόθον καὶ τὸν Ὑμέναιον ἔτι πρὸς τούτοις παραλήψομαι.

ΠΑΡΙΣ: Οὐκοῦν ἐπὶ τούτοις δίδωμι τὸ μῆλον: ἐπὶ τούτοις λάμβανε.

ἄγω: to lead or bring
ἀκολουθέω: to follow
ἀφικνέομαι: to come to, arrive
δίδωμι: to give
θαρρέω: to be of good courage
Ἴλιος, ἡ: Ilios, the city of Troy
λαμβάνω: to take
μηδαμῶς: not at all
οὐκοῦν: therefore, then

πάλιν: again
παραδίδωμι: to give over
παραλαμβάνω: to take along
πάρειμι: to be presesnt
Πόθος, ὁ: Longing
συμπράττω: to help in doing
Ὑμέναιος, ὁ: Hymen, god of marriage
ὑπισχνέομαι: to promise
Χάριται, αἱ: the Graces

ὑπόσχου: aor. imper. of ὑπο-ισχνέομαι, "promise!"
παρέσομαι: fut., "I will be alongside"
συμπράξω: fut., "I will manage"
ἄξεις: fut., "will you bring?"
παραλήψομαι: fut. of παρα-λαμβάνω, "I will take along"
ἐπὶ τούτοις: "on these conditions"

List of Verbs

List of Verbs

The following is a list of verbs that have some irregularity in their conjugation. Contract verbs and other verbs that are completely predictable (-ίζω, -εύω, etc.) are generally not included. The principal parts of the Greek verb in order are 1. Present 2. Future 3. Aorist 4. Perfect Active 5. Perfect Middle 6. Aorist Passive, 7. Future Passive. We have not included the future passive below, since it is very rare. For many verbs not all forms are attested or are only poetic. Verbs are alphabetized under their main stem, followed by various compounds that occur in the *Judgment of the Goddesses* with a brief definition. A dash (-) before a form means that it occurs only or chiefly with a prefix. The list is based on the list of verbs in H. Smyth, *A Greek Grammar*.

ἄγω: to lead ἄξω, 2 aor. ἤγαγον, ἦχα, ἦγμαι, ἤχθην
   μετάγω: to transfer

αἰνέω: to praise -αινέσω, -ήνεσα, -ήνεκα, -ήνημαι, -ηνέθην.
   ἐπαινέω: to approve, praise

αἱρέω: to take αἱρήσω, 2 aor. εἷλον, ᾕρηκα, ᾕρημαι, ᾑρέθην
   ἀφαιρέω: to take from

ἀκούω: to hear ἀκούσομαι, ἤκουσα, 2 perf. ἀκήκοα, ἠκούσθην

ἀπαντάω: to meet ἀπαντήσομαι, ἀπήντησα, ἀπήντηκα.

ἀρέσκω: to please: ἀρέσω, ἤρεσα; mid. ἀρέσκομαι appease: ἀρέσομαι, ἠρεσάμην, ἠρέσθην.

ἁρπάζω: to snatch away ἁρπάσομαι, ἥρπασα, ἥρπακα, ἥρπασμαι, ἡρπάσθην

ἀφικνέομαι: to arrive at ἀφ-ίξομαι, 2 aor. ἀφ-ικόμην, ἀφ-ῖγμαι

ἄχθομαι: to be vexed ἀχθέσομαι, ἠχθέσθην

βαίνω: to step βήσομαι, 2 aor. ἔβην, βέβηκα
   καταβαίνω: to go down
   μεταβαίνω: to pass over from one place to another
   συμβαίνω: to come together, come to pass

βάλλω: to throw βαλῶ, 2 aor. ἔβαλον, βέβληκα, βέβλημαι, ἐβλήθην
   ἀποβάλλω: to throw away, shed, lose
   περιβάλλω: to throw around, put on

βλέπω: to look at βλέψομαι, ἔβλεψα
   ἀποβλέπω: to look upon, regard, attend

βούλομαι: to wish βουλήσομαι, βεβούλημαι, ἐβουλήθην

γι(γ)νώσκω: to know γνώσομαι, ἔγνων, ἔγνωκα, ἔγνωσμαι, ἐγνώσθην
   ἀναγιγνώσκω: to read

γί(γ)νομαι: to become γενήσομαι, 2 aor. ἐγενόμην, 2 perf. γέγονα,
   γεγένημαι, ἐγενήθην

δείκνυμι: to show δείξω, ἔδειξα, δέδειχα, δέδειγμαι, ἐδείχθην
   ἐπιδείκνυμι: to show, exhibit

δέομαι: to want, ask: δεήσομαι, δεδέημαι, ἐδεήθην.

δέχομαι: to receive δέξομαι, ἐδεξάμην, δέδεγμαι, -εδέχθην

δίδωμι: to give δώσω, 1 aor. ἔδωκα in s., 2 aor. ἔδομεν in pl. δέδωκα,
   δέδομαι, ἐδόθην
   ἀποδίδωμι: to give back, return, render
   παραδίδωμι: to give over

δοκέω: to think, seem δόξω, ἔδοξα, δέδογμαι
   συνδοκέω: to seem good also, agree

ἐθέλω: to wish ἐθελήσω, ἠθέλησα, ἠθέληκα

εἶδον: to see (aor.); see ὁράω

εἰμί: to be, ἔσομαι, impf. ἦν
   ἄπειμι: to be absent
   πάρειμι: to be present, stand by
   πρόσειμι: to be present
   συμπάρειμι: to be present with, be together
   σύνειμι: to be with

εἶπον: to say (aor.); see λέγω

εἴργω: to shut in or out εἴρξω, εἶρξα, εἴργμαι, εἴρχθην
   ἀνείργω: to keep back, restrain

ἐλέγχω: to examine, confute: ἐλέγξω, ἤλεγξα, ἐλήλεγμαι, ἠλέγχθην

ἕπομαι: to follow ἕψομαι, 2 aor. ἑσπόμην

ἐράω: to love, imp. ἤρων aor. ἠράσθην

ἐργάζομαι: to work, ἐργάσομαι, ἠργασάμην, εἴργασμαι, ἠργάσθην
    ἀπεργάζομαι: to finish off, work to completion

ἔρχομαι: to come or go to: fut. εἶμι, 2 aor. ἦλθον, 2 perf. ἐλήλυθα
    ἐπανέρχομαι: to return
    ἐπέρχομαι: to approach
    κατέρχομαι: to go down
    παρέρχομαι: to go beside

ἐρωτάω: to ask ἐρήσομαι, 2 aor. ἠρόμην

ἔχω: to have ἕξω, 2 aor. ἔσχον, ἔσχηκα, imperf. εἶχον
    ἐπέχω: to hold back
    παρέχω: to furnish, provide, supply
    προσέχω: to hold to, be devoted to

ἡγέομαι: to go before, lead the way ἡγήσομαι, ἡγησάμην, ἥγημαι
    διηγέομαι: to set out in detail, describe in full

ἦλθον: to go (*aor.*) see ἔρχομαι

ἵστημι: to make to stand, set στήσω shall set, ἔστησα set, caused to stand, 2
    aor. ἔστην stood, 1 perf. ἔστηκα stand, plupf. εἱστήκη stood, ἐστάθην
    ἀφίστημι: to put away, remove
    ἐφίστημι: to set upon
    καθίστημι: to set down, place
    παρίστημι: to stand up beside

καλέω: to call καλῶ, ἐκάλεσα, κέκληκα, κέκλημαι, ἐκλήθην
    ἐγκαλέω: to reproach

κρίνω: to decide κρινῶ, ἔκρινα, κέκρικα, κέκριμαι, ἐκρίθην
    ἀποκρίνω: to answer
    προκρίνω: to choose before others, prefer

λαμβάνω: to take λήψομαι, ἔλαβον, εἴληφα, εἴλημμαι, ἐλήφθην
    παραλαμβάνω: to take beside
    περιλαμβάνω: embrace

λάμπω: to shine λάμψω, ἔλαμψα, λέλαμπα, -λέλησμαι
    ἀπολάμπω: to shine or beam from

λέγω: to speak ἐρέω, εἶπον, εἴρηκα, λέλεγμαι, ἐλέχθην and ἐρρήθην

λείπω: to leave λείψω, ἔλιπον, λέλοιπα, λέλειμμαι, ἐλείφθην
    ἀπολείπω: to leave behind

Lucian

μανθάνω: to learn μαθήσομαι, ἔμαθον, μεμάθηκα

μέμφομαι: to blame μέμψομαι, ἐμεμψάμην, ἐμέμφθην

μένω: to stay μενῶ, ἔμεινα, μεμένηκα
    παραμένω: to stay beside, remain with
    περιμένω: to wait for, await

μιμνῄσκω: to remind, remember (mid.). -μνήσω, -έμνησα, perf. μέμνημαι
    (with present sense), ἐμνήσθην

νέμω: to distribute νεμῶ, ἔνειμα, -νενέμηκα, νενέμημαι, ἐνεμήθην

οἴομαι: or οἶμαι: to suppose ᾠήθην imperf. ᾤμην

ὄμνυμι: to swear ὀμοῦμαι, ὤμοσα, ὀμώμοκα, ὀμώμομαι, ὠμόθην
    ἐπόμνυμι: to swear upon

ὁράω: to see ὄψομαι, 2 aor. εἶδον, ἑώρακα, ὤφθην, imperf. ἑώρων

ὀρέγω: to reach ὀρέξω, ὤρεξα, ὠρέχθην

πάσχω: to experience πείσομαι, 2 aor. ἔπαθον, 2 perf. πέπονθα

πείθω: to persuade πείσω, ἔπεισα, 2 perf. πέποιθα, πέπεισμαι, ἐπείσθην
    ἀναπείθω: to persuade, convince

πέμπω: to convey πέμψω, ἔπεμψα, 2 perf. πέπομφα, πέπεμμαι, ἐπέμφθην
    καταπέμπω: to send down

περαίνω: to accomplish: περανῶ, ἐπέρανα, πεπέρασμαι

πέτομαι: to fly πτήσομαι, 2 aor. -επτόμην
    καταπέτομαι: to fly down

πλέω: to sail πλεύσομαι, ἔπλευσα, πέπλευκα, πέπλευσμαι, ἐπλεύσθην
    συνεκπλέω: to sail out along with

πράττω: to do πράξω, ἔπραξα, 2 perf. πέπραχα, πέπραγμαι, ἐπράχθην
    καταπράττω: to accomplish, arrange
    συμπράττω: to help in doing

σπάω: to draw σπάσω, ἔσπασα, -έσπακα, ἔσπασμαι, -εσπάσθην
    ἀποσπάω: to tear or drag away from
    περισπάω: to draw away from

στέλλω: to send, arrange στελῶ, ἔστειλα, -έσταλκα, ἔσταλμαι, ἐστάλην
    ἀποστέλλω: to send off or away from

στρέφω: to turn στρέψω, ἔστρεψα, ἔστραμμαι, ἐστρέφθην
  ἀποστρέφω: to turn around, turn back

ταράττω: to stir up ταράξω, ἐτάραξα, τετάραγμαι, ἐταράχθην

τάττω: to arrange, τάξω, ἔταξα, 2 perf. τέταχα, τέταγμαι, ἐτάχθην
  προστάττω: to arrange

τίθημι: to place θήσω, ἔθηκα, τέθηκα, τέθειμαι (but usu. κεῖμαι), ἐτέθην
  ἀποτίθημι: to put away
  ἐπιτίθημι: to put upon, add to

τρέπω: to turn τρέψω, ἔτρεψα, τέτροφα, ἐτράπην
  ἐπιτρέπω: to turn towards

τρέφω: to nourish θρέψω, ἔθρεψα, 2 perf. τέτροφα, τέθραμμαι, ἐτράφην

τρέχω: to run δραμοῦμαι, ἔδραμον, -δεδράμηκα
  παρατρέχω: to run by or past

τρίβω: to rub τρίψω, ἔτριψα, 2 perf. τέτριφα, τέτριμμαι, ἐτρίβην
  ἐνδιατρίβω: to spend time in
  ἐντρίβω: to rub in or into

τυγχάνω: to happen τεύξομαι, ἔτυχον, τετύχηκα. τέτυγμαι, ἐτύχθην

ὑπισχνέομαι: to promise ὑπο-σχήσομαι, 2 aor. ὑπ-εσχόμην

φαίνω: to show, to appear (mid.) φανῶ, ἔφηνα, πέφηνα, πέφασμαι, ἐφάνην

φέρω: to bear οἴσω, 1 aor. ἤνεγκα, 2 aor. ἤνεγκον, 2 perf. ἐνήνοχα, perf.
  mid. ἐνήνεγμαι, aor. pass. ἠνέχθην
  ἀναφέρω: to bring or carry up

φημί: to say φήσω, ἔφησα

φθείρω: to corrupt: φθερῶ, ἔφθειρα, 2 perf. -έφθορα am ruined, ἔφθαρμαι, 2
  aor. pass. ἐφθάρην.
  διαφθείρω: to destroy utterly

χαίρω: to rejoice at χαιρήσω, κεχάρηκα, κεχάρημαι, ἐχάρην

χαλεπαίνω: to be offended χαλεπανῶ, ἐχαλέπηνα, ἐχαλεπάνθην

χέω: to pour fut. χέω, aor. ἔχεα, κέχυκα, κέχυμαι, ἐχύθην
  περιχέω: to pour round or over

Glossary

Α α

ἀγαθός, -ή, -όν: good

ἄγω: to lead or carry, to convey, bring

ἀεί: always

ἀκούω: to hear

ἀληθής, -ές: unconcealed, true

ἀλλά: otherwise, but

ἄλλως: in another way

ἅμα: at the same time

ἄν: (*indefinite particle; generalizes dependent clauses with subjunctive; indicates contrary-to-fact with independent clauses in the indicative; potentiality with the optative*)

ἅπας, ἅπασα, ἅπαν: all, the whole

ἀπό: from, away from (+ gen.)

αὐτός, -ή, -ό: he, she, it; self, same

Γ γ

γάρ: for

γε: at least, at any rate (*postpositive*)

γί(γ)νομαι: to become, happen, occur

γι(γ)νώσκω: to know

γυνή, γυναικός, ἡ: a woman

Δ δ

δέ: and, but, on the other hand (*preceded by* μέν)

δεῖ: it is necessary

δή: certainly, now (postpositive)

διά: through (+ gen.); with, by means of (+ acc.)

δίδωμι: to give

δικαστής, -οῦ, ὁ: a judge

δοκέω: to seem

δύναμαι: to be able (+ inf.)

δύο: two

Ε ε

ἐγώ, μοῦ, μοί, μέ: I, my, me

ἐθέλω: to will, wish, purpose

εἰ: if

εἶδον: to see (*aor.*)

εἰμί: to be

εἶμι: to go (*fut.*) see ἔρχομαι

εἰς, ἐς: into, to (+ *acc.*)

εἷς, μία, ἕν: one

ἐκ, ἐξ: from, out of, after (+ *gen.*)

ἕκαστος, -η, -ον: each, every

ἐκεῖνος, -η, -ον: that, that one

ἐμός, -ή, -όν: my, mine

ἐν: in, at, among (+ *dat.*)

ἕνεκα: for the sake of (+ *gen.*)

ἔοικα: to seem, to be like (*perf.*)

ἐπεί: since

ἐπί: at (+ *gen.*); on, upon (+ *dat.*); on to, against (+ *acc.*)

ἐρωτάω: to ask, enquire

ἔτι: still

εὖ: well, thoroughly

ἔχω: to have; to be able (+ *inf.*)

Η η

ἤ: or; than

ἤδη: already, now

ἡμεῖς, ἡμῶν, ἡμᾶς, ἡμῖν: we, us

Θ θ

θεά, ἡ: a goddess

θέα, ἡ: a seeing

Ι ι

ἵνα: in order that (+ *subj.*)

ἴσος, -η, -ον: equal to, the same as

Κ κ

καί: and, also, even

κακός, -ή, -όν: bad, cowardly

45

κάλλος, -ους, τό: beauty

καλός, -ή, όν: good

κατά, καθ': down, along, according to (+ acc.)

κελεύω: to command, order

κρίσις, ἡ: a judgment, decision

Λ λ

λαμβάνω: to take

λέγω: to speak, say, tell

λόγος, ὁ: a word

Μ μ

μέν: on the one hand (followed by δέ)

μέγας, μέγαλα, μέγα: great, large

μετά: with (+ gen.); after (+ acc.)

μή: not, lest, don't (+ subj. or imper.)

μηδέ: but not, and not, nor

μῆλον, τό; an apple

μόνος, -η, -ον: alone, only

Ν ν

νῦν: now, at this moment

Ο ο

ὁ, ἡ, τό: the (definite article)

ὅδε, ἥδε, τόδε: this

οἶδα: to know (perf.)

οἴομαι: to suppose, think, deem, imagine

οἷος, -α, -ον: such as, what sort

ὅλος, -η, -ον: whole, entire

ὅπως: as, in such manner as, how

ὁράω: to see

ὅστις, ὅτι: anyone who, anything which

ὅτι: that, because

οὐ, οὐκ, οὐχ: not

οὐδέ: but not

οὖν: so, therefore

οὗτος, αὕτη, τοῦτο: this

οὕτως: in this way

Π π

παῖς, παιδός, ὁ: a child

παρά: from (+ gen.); beside (+ dat.); to (+ acc.)

περί: concerning, about (+ gen.); about, around (+ acc.)

πλήν: unless, but

ποιέω: to make, do

πολλάκις: many times, often

πολύς, πολλή, πολύ: many, much

πρός: to, near (+ dat.), from (+ gen.), towards (+ acc.)

πρότερος, -α, -ον: prior, earlier

πρῶτος, -η, -ον: first

πῶς: how? in what way?

Σ σ

σύ, σοῦ, σέ, σοί: you (singular)

Τ τ

τε: and (postpositive)

τις, τι: someone, something (indefinite)

τίς, τί: who? which? (interrogative)

τοιοῦτος, -αύτη, -οῦτο: such as this

τότε: at that time, then

τυγχάνω: to hit upon, happen

Υ υ

ὑμεῖς, ὑμῶν, ὑμᾶς, ὑμῖν: you (pl.)

ὑπό: from under, by (+ gen.); under (+ dat.); toward (+ acc.)

Φ φ

φημί: to say

Χ χ

χρή: it is necessary

Ω ω

ὡς: (*adv.*) as, so, how; (*conj.*) that, in
order that, since; (*prep.*) to (+ *acc.*);
as if, as (+ *part.*); as _____ as possible
(+ *superlative*)

ὥσπερ: just as

ὥστε: so that, and so

ὦ: O! (*vocative*)

NOTES

NOTES

NOTES

NOTES

Printed in the USA
CPSIA information can be obtained
at www.ICGtesting.com
LVHW011241230823
756032LV00004B/245